OUR LADY'S PSALTER

Ave
Maria
Gratia
Plena
Dominus
Tecum

Benedicta
Tu in
Mulieribus
et
Benedictus
Fructus
Ventris tui
Iesus

PRAISE FOR *Our Lady's Psalter*

"This rare book, *Our Lady's Psalter: Reflections on the Mysteries of the Traditional Rosary* by Fr. Robert Bradley, S.J., provides a profound, insightful exploration of the Joyful, Sorrowful, and Glorious Mysteries of the Virgin Mary. Our Lady's heart, her mother's love radiates from these pages. This fruit of Fr. Bradley's lifelong contemplation of the Blessed Mother provides a mystical feast, a window into heaven, and a practical means of walking with Mary in a way that changes lives. I pray that the Holy Spirit will carry Fr. Bradley's writing into all Catholic homes to bless and fortify. Highly recommended."

—KATHLEEN BECKMAN, D.H.S., Co-Founder, Foundation of Prayer for Priests; author of *Praying for Priests: An Urgent Call for the Salvation of Souls*

"Fr. Robert I. Bradley, S.J. was one of the finest priests I ever met. His niece, Betty Bosarge, OSF, has done the Catholic world a great favor in editing these profound reflections on the Joyful, Sorrowful, and Glorious Mysteries of the Holy Rosary. Fr. Bradley penetrates into the deeper meaning of these Mysteries and how they embrace the whole of salvation history. Drawing upon the insights of St. Ignatius of Loyola, he shows how these Mysteries illuminate not only the life of the Virgin Mary but also those of St. Joseph, St. John the Apostle, St. Peter, and St. Paul. These reflections have a poetic quality, and can serve as a rich resource for homilies and personal meditation. Those reading this book will understand why Pope Pius XII referred to the Rosary as 'the compendium of the entire Gospel.'"

—ROBERT FASTIGGI, Professor of Dogmatic Theology, Sacred Heart Seminary, Detroit

"Fr. Robert Bradley, who helped found Catholics United for the Faith and was an outstanding theologian, offers a beautiful meditation on each HAIL MARY of the traditional fifteen Mysteries of the Holy Rosary. I know of no other commentary like it. It should be in the hands of every Catholic, especially during the Lenten season."

—FR. DONALD CALLOWAY, MIC, author of *Champions of the Rosary*

"In *Our Lady's Psalter,* Fr. Bradley shows himself to be a true spiritual master after Our Lady's own heart. Through the meditations of his powerful book, the scholar-priest enhances the Mysteries of the Holy Rosary in a way that makes them more approachable and understandable to us all. When surrounded by such rich meditations, the Rosary begs to be prayed. Fr. Bradley has truly given us all a gift! I encourage everyone who wants to love the Lord Jesus through Mary to pick up and zealously use this spiritual treasury!"

—FR. JEFFREY KIRBY, STD, author of *Glory Unto Glory*

"I am thrilled that this book, which I have known about for decades, is finally seeing the light of day. There are a multitude of valuable meditations on the Holy Rosary—but even so, *Our Lady's Psalter* stands out. There is simply no other work like it. And it comes from one of the unsung heroes of the post-conciliar Church in America, the brilliant, humble, and ever-faithful Fr. Robert Bradley, SJ."

—MICHAEL P. FOLEY, author of *Lost in Translation: Meditating on the Orations of the Traditional Roman Rite*

OUR LADY'S PSALTER

REFLECTIONS ON
THE MYSTERIES OF THE
TRADITIONAL ROSARY

FR. ROBERT I. BRADLEY, S.J.

Angelico Press

For information, address:
Angelico Press, Ltd.
169 Monitor St.
Brooklyn, NY 11222
www.angelicopress.com

ppr 979-8-89280-092-1
cloth 979-8-89280-093-8
ebook 979-8-89280-094-5

Book and cover design
by Michael Schrauzer

FOREWORD

WITH joy and gratitude we welcome this volume of Rosary meditations composed by Fr. Robert I. Bradley, S.J., and assembled by his devoted editor of many years, Betty Bosarge, O.S.F., in the months following his death in December 2013. Fr. Bradley served as our chaplain from 1987 to 1996 and nourished us daily with the Word and the Bread of Life. His homilies, pertinent to the feast or the day's readings, provided rich fare for his "little brown sparrows," as he often called us because of our Franciscan Poor Clare habit.

We also benefited from some of the classes he was conducting at the Notre Dame Catechetical Institute (now the Notre Dame Graduate School of Christendom College). He generously offered the same classes for us in our parlor.

Even in the early 1990s, the idea of these meditations on the Rosary was stirring in his heart, and Father shared some of the first ones with us. This book is a rich treasure of his distilled thought and prayer, and a valuable aid for growing in the spiritual life and in devotion to "our Blessed Lady," as he loved to call her.

These short meditations, one for each Hail Mary of the original fifteen decades of the Rosary, flesh out the mysteries with a blending of tradition and Christian piety, and create a spiritual atmosphere in which to immerse our Marian prayer. Fr. Bradley's inimitable way of turning a phrase, adding a "light" touch, or ending with a provocative question engages the mind as well as the heart, making one look forward to the next meditation.

Betty Bosarge, herself an accomplished writer, has done a beautiful work in bringing these meditations to the public. We thank her for not "just another book of Rosary meditations," but a sure companion on the way.

The Poor Clare Nuns
Alexandria, VA

PREFACE

WRITING these miniature essays/meditations in *Our Lady's Psalter* was a long but fruitful journey for Fr. Robert Ignatius Bradley, S.J. Guided by the Holy Spirit and our Blessed Mother, he began this journey in 1995 and continued through 2006, ever faithful and always listening to the heavenly voices speaking to his heart and soul.

Deeply devoted to our Blessed Mother since childhood, Fr. Bradley prayed three Rosaries daily, eventually adding a fourth with the Luminous Mysteries. The Holy Spirit spoke to him as he prayed and meditated. He began to write down his prayerful and often scholarly thoughts for each bead, eventually finding himself with 150 hand-written reflections on a stack of yellow legal pads. So began *Our Lady's Psalter*, reflections on the traditional Rosary of the Joyful, Sorrowful, and Glorious Mysteries.

When Pope St. John Paul II proclaimed the Luminous Mysteries in 2002, Fr. Bradley wanted to write reflections on them after finishing the traditional three. But his other duties as a priest for the Traditional Latin Mass in Austin, Texas, his work as a professor of theology for graduate students and seminarians, and his other labors as a retreat master, conference speaker, and chaplain to various organizations kept him from putting pen to paper. Then illness set in as he reached his mid-eighties, and he found himself unable to write. Even his voluminous correspondence with friends all over the world became a struggle for him. In the end, he was not able to commit his reflections on the Luminous Mysteries to paper.

For all of his life, Fr. Bradley struggled with writing and blamed this on his "problem of perfectionism." But when he did finish writing an article, book, sermon, class handout, or letter, the writing was exquisite, a unique style that was oftentimes very beautiful in the way he expressed his thoughts. He would point out that he was not a writer; indeed, writing was a major task for him that often left him anguished with wadded-up drafts piled around him. Instead, he was a teacher, conveying the Faith in his homilies and to his graduate students and seminarians, to groups of Catholics who attended his presentations at retreats, conferences, and lectures throughout the nation. He was most "at home" on the altar, in the confessional, and in the classroom.

He found computers to be strange inventions that were not for him, although he did make some valiant attempts at learning to operate them. Thus, all his work was handwritten or typed on an ancient portable typewriter from his high school days in the 1930s. Although his handwriting was small and difficult to read, those fortunate enough to receive his many letters through the years rejoiced at the wisdom he imparted to them, whether it be to help them solve a problem or simply to give them some spiritual nourishment.

He wanted to share these Rosary reflections with everyone: his large family of friends, former students, fellow priests, parishioners, and the future generations of Catholics who come to love Our Lady—everyone who has a heart and soul open to hearing the voice of the triune God.

Fr. Bradley considered these short essays to be his personal lifelong love letter to our Blessed Mother, reflections that sprang from the depths of his soul and were wrapped in the love abundant in his heart.

It is an honor for me to have assisted Father with his writing for over thirty years. May these reflections be a blessing and bring abundant grace to all who study them.

Dr. Betty B. Bosarge, O. S. F.
Editor for Fr. Robert I. Bradley, S. J.
February 2025

MODERN DAY POPES
and
THE HOLY ROSARY

A QUEST FOR PEACE
IN THE WORLD

O UR Blessed Lady holds a prime position in the teachings of Saint Pope Paul VI and his successors in the Chair of Peter. That position is absolutely central to the papal teachings, for she is simply central to the Church.

"Mother of the Church" is the title Pope Paul has given her. But in so doing, he has said nothing new. He has but reaffirmed the tradition of the Faith, received from his predecessors and readied for his successors. In a sense, as the Second Vatican Council profoundly senses (and particularly in its greatest document, the *Constitution on the Church*), that is all that really need be said. If Mary is Mother — Mother of Christ and Mother of us — then that says it all. What remains is simply to live what that says.

But as in life there are echoes, reverberations of unique and indivisible experience caught up into a rhythm of a total experience — itself echoing the point-by-point pattern of our earthly lives, from breath to breath, from heartbeat to heartbeat, and echoing in turn the point-by-point pattern of the universe: the cadence of sunlight and starlight, the recurrence of the seasons, and all the known motions of the celestial spheres — so today we may indulge in an echo of the holy words we hear about Our Lady. After all, the words of the Holy Fathers over the centuries about Our

Lady and her Rosary are themselves but echoes: repetitions of what they first heard as little children from their mothers. As all mothers and all children surely know, the words between them tend to be repetitive.

The Rosary is the Church's repetitive prayer *par excellence* to the Mother of God, the prayer that has been the object of her repetitive exhortations to her children through so many centuries, and now in our own times more than ever before.

Did you know that in these last hundred and fifty years more papal encyclicals have been written on the Holy Rosary than on any other subject? Leo XIII alone spoke to the whole Catholic world on the Rosary no less than eleven times! All his great messages — on the social and political order, on Scriptural and philosophical studies, on the specific needs of the Church in the various countries of the Old and New Worlds — all were gathered up, as it were, in the one encompassing vision of the reality of God and his Christ that he saw best mediated to all the Catholic faithful in the mysteries of that same Christ and his Mother that we have in the Rosary.

The successors of Pope Leo maintained this same view. Under the aegis of Mary, St. Pius X would restore all things in Christ and Benedict XV would reconcile a world at war. It was during his pontificate, you will remember, that three peasant children on the edge of Europe saw in immediate vision what the three popes — Leo, Pius, and Benedict — saw only in reasoned faith: peace, true peace, could come only from heaven, just as the Lady had come — with a Rosary in her hands.

When, a year later, the guns were stilled, the world finally had its peace — negative, fitful, and fraught with future disaster. To this world Pius XI offered "the peace of Christ in the reign of Christ"; and he told the world that if it would have this peace — the only sure and positive peace it could ever have — it must pray for it. And the prayer of the Catholic faithful must be the Rosary.

Ingravescentibus Malis was the significant title of his encyclical on the Rosary, dated September 1937—one year before Munich. The armistice that the world had called "peace" could no longer contain the evils that had been growing all along; and so war came again.

Pius XII (as did how many others among us?) thought that surely the ordeal of World War II would bring a different peace this time, and in 1948 he called on us to pray the Rosary to speed this peace. He called his encyclical *Auspicia Quaedam*; humbled and hopeful, the world would surely this time beg Christ's peace and receive it. But again, the prayer was too little and too late. And three years later, while Korea was aflame, the Holy Father wrote his second encyclical on the Rosary, *Ingruentium Malorum.* Again, the title says it. The terrible evils in this world would tear it asunder unless justice is established, for from justice alone comes peace.

We know, dear friends, what the sequel has been. The horrors have been compounded, and the peace we seek is farther away than ever. Pope St. John XXIII in his inimitable manner reminisced in 1959 in his encyclical *Grata Recordatio* on the great Leonine series on the Rosary that he remembered as a boy; and quietly he urged again what had been urged for so long, if our century would ever have peace.

Then, in the 1960s, bent under the scourge of the Vietnam War, we heard (or did we hear?) Blessed Pope Paul speak out in his turn on this same theme, in his encyclical *Christi Matri* (September 1966). The world press (including the greater part of the Catholic press), used as it unfortunately is to the inflation of cheap rhetoric, heard only a negative lament, only one more voice in the chorus of pacifist dissent. What they did not hear was the positive word of Pope Paul—typically strong and substantive, brief and profound. What the Holy Father was saying was that peace is the gift of God and we must pray for it!

Because he was not heard, with typical patience he repeated his words. Three years later, in an apostolic exhortation entitled *Recurrens Mensis October*, he told us yet once more: if we are to have real peace, we must really pray. And a real prayer, within the reach of all of us and enriched by the example of the saints who have gone before us, is the Holy Rosary of the Blessed Virgin Mary.

Yes, this succession of papal proclamations is singularly impressive. In the consistency of its persistence, it easily ranks with those earlier recurring instances of rare magnitude — like the conversion of the barbarians and the crusade against the infidel — where the Holy See has dramatized, as it were, the plight of earth, the remedy of heaven, and the mediating mission of the Church. In all these instances, paradoxical in some of them but profoundly real in all, the world's plight has been its lack of peace: the only true peace that is Christ's. For peace is the fulfillment of justice, the tranquility of order, the first fruits of paradise, the only heaven this side of heaven that this poor earth can ever have.

That is why Blessed Pope Paul speaks of peace, to the seeming exclusion of all other matters. And that is why, too, he speaks to us, to the seeming exclusion of those extensions of people we call "institutions." For all these institutions, or structures, on which we build our hopes for peace and which we blame if we do not have it — for government, for the military, for the economy, for the academy, for the media — for all these things Pope Paul has scarcely a word. He considers them, in a sense, irrelevant.

What is relevant, and indeed radical here, is the human will, where alone reside the values that are moral: the good that is the justice and order we speak of, or the evil that is their privation. Peace begins and ends, then, in the human heart! If peace is not there, no seeming "peace" in the world, however it be proclaimed or packaged, can compensate. But if peace is there, then all the warfare in the world can never be total and will someday be doomed.

Now Pope Paul, in perfect continuity with his predecessors, insists that prayer is the primary means to peace. Surely, in the light of what we have just now seen, you must see why this is so. If peace is essentially personal justice in the moral order, then what destroys and prevents peace is sin. And what alone remits sin and protects us from it is the merciful grace of God. This grace we ask for, and we do that by prayer. Prayer to God and to his Christ, the Sun of Justice and the Prince of Peace: this is what we must do!

But, by both the experience of nature and the instinct of grace, we do this — how? Not immediately, lest that divinity's sunlight blind us and its principality overwhelm us. Rather, we seek him in the same way he sought us: through the mediation of a creature he chose — Holy Mary, the Woman who "humanized" God! And so we pray: "Holy Mary, Mother of God, pray for us sinners — now." And since there is a new moment and a new "now," and always so until we die, we repeat this prayer. It must be as tirelessly prayed, as we can be sure it is tirelessly heard. For now she hears us, and now God hears her!

Prayer, the simple, humble prayer of petition: this is what the Rosary provides; and blessed are we if we use it. Indeed, our blessing will consist in part of a new awareness of a greater dimension to prayer, surpassing petition. For the Rosary can school us in that second and higher prayer we call reflection or meditation: think about what I can and should do, what I can and should be, after the example of what Jesus and his Mother do and are.

Here, moreover, is an inbuilt corrective to the ever-present possibility of imperfect petitionary prayer. Should such prayer make me less "responsible," more "mechanical," putting off on God or Our Lady what I can and should do myself, then let me reflect, either on the words I pronounce or on the mysteries I ponder — the Rosary gives me both. I should see myself, then, in this light of life that is his Life before me. In my present pains and pleasures, I should think of how he was then in his joys and sorrows, and I will think of my future as he is now, in his glory.

Yes, the Rosary is perfect meditative prayer. In it, I not only speak to Our Lady, but she speaks to me. I hear her repeat to me now her last recorded words: "Whatever he shall say to you, do!" Here is quintessentially the Christian school, for here both the Master and the lesson are Christ.

This would surely be enough to justify the exhortations of all recent popes, from Leo XIII to Francis, that we fervently pray the Rosary. But no, dear friends, there is actually a further step to take: a third and higher kind of prayer awaits us in the Rosary. This is indeed the highest prayer that with ordinary grace we are capable of: the prayer of contemplation.

To contemplation meditative prayer spontaneously leads, and by contemplation ultimately it is correctly maintained. For just as petition can become disordered, so too can meditation. It can become self-centered, losing its only true orientation, which is beyond self and to Christ.

This true orderer of prayer, this true peacemaker of our soul, is what we call contemplation. We see no longer ourselves but only Jesus; we lose ourselves in his mysteries or in the words of his angels and saints. His mysteries — joyful, luminous, sorrowful, glorious — are now just that: they are now! His birth or his agony are no longer past events I reflect upon for some lesson to myself. Rather, they are present realities that I contemplate. And what I see and hear and touch is always him: the Lord in whose presence all else fades away. I am still there, of course, for he beholds me, and that beholding by my Creator and Redeemer is all I need. Thus, there is no longer need for petition or meditation as such. He knows already, and better than I can ever know, what I can do by my own resolution and what I must simply ask that he do for me. Prayer becomes so simple then; and the simplest prayer of all is the Rosary!

Indeed, so simple is it, that in the Rosary we can always go back — and occasionally we should — to those previous "lesser" ways of prayer. There are certainly enough "Aves" for this variety! And so the rhythms of the Rosary admit of endless modulation: an ageless echoing, in human words and earthly happenings, of the celestial prayer of the angels — that perfect dynamism of adoring love that is the ultimate justice and the eternal order for which we were made, the peace in which our restless hearts will finally rest.

These few thoughts of peace and prayer and the Rosary I offer you, dear friends, as but echoes of the teachings of our bishops, and especially of our Holy Fathers the popes. Singly, regionally, and in general council, our bishops have reaffirmed for our times "the practices and exercises of devotion to the most Blessed Virgin Mary which have been recommended for centuries by the Magisterium of the Church."*

Following the Second Vatican Council, the exercise of that Magisterium by Saint Paul VI has been, as we have already seen, in perfect harmony with his predecessors. Surely, enough has been explicitly and officially stated, not to mention implicit or unofficial statements, to warrant a real renewal of the Rosary as the singular, privileged prayer of our times.

And what about Pope Paul's successors and the Holy Rosary? Prior to his very short pontificate, John Paul I, as Albino Cardinal Luciani in a 1973 homily entitled "My Rosary," responded to critics who were calling

---

* *Lumen Gentium* 67; see also the two paragraphs devoted to the Rosary in the pastoral letter by the American bishops, "Behold Your Mother," 96–97.

the Rosary "an impoverished prayer": "The Rosary is an impoverished prayer? What then would be a 'rich prayer'? The Rosary is a procession of Paters, the prayer taught by Jesus; of Aves, the salutation of God to the Virgin by means of the angel; of Glorias, the praise of the Most Holy Trinity.... The crisis of the Rosary doesn't come first. What comes first is the crisis in prayer in general today. People are all taken up in material interests; they think little about the soul... for the interior life, and for... the tender colloquy with God, ... it is too tiring to find a few minutes of time. What a pity!... The Rosary, a simple and easy prayer, helps me to be a child again, and I am not ashamed of it at all."

A powerful homily indeed! And his successor, St. John Paul II, followed with many exhortations to the people of God to pray the Rosary daily. So faithful was this saint in his own daily recitations of the Holy Rosary that in 2002 he added an additional Mystery — the Luminous — to bring us even closer to the life of Jesus in prayer.

The Holy Father had a deep devotion to the Blessed Mother going back to his childhood in Poland. He had a Marian cross in his coat of arms and made more Marian pilgrimages than any of his predecessors. During his long pontificate, he wrote several encyclicals to shape the Church's views on Mary in this modern age. Among the greatest encyclicals on Mary is *Redemptoris Mater*, Mother of the Redeemer, proclaimed in 1987, which taught that Mary has a specific role in God's plan of salvation.

In 2002, St. John Paul wrote an apostolic letter, *Rosarium Virginis Mariae*, in which he explained his total consecration to Mary, inspired by St. Louis de Montfort, and said he chose his motto, *Totus Tuus*, as a reminder of how a life centered in Jesus Christ leads to total consecration to the Blessed Virgin Mary as our Mother.

So too did Pope Benedict XVI have a deep devotion to the Blessed Mother and daily recitation of the Rosary. In

October 2012 he asked Catholics throughout the world to "rediscover the Rosary" in the forthcoming Year of Faith. In his Sunday Angelus comments on October 7, the Pope told the pilgrims assembled in St. Peter's Square: "With the Rosary, we allow ourselves to be guided by Mary, model of faith, in meditating on the mysteries of Christ, and day after day we are helped to assimilate the Gospel, so that it shapes all our lives."

Reflecting on the apostolic letter *Rosarium Virginis Mariae*, the pope invited the pilgrims "to pray the Rosary personally, in the family, and in the community, learning at the school of Mary, which leads us to Christ, the living center of our faith."

Pope Francis, too, tells us about his devotion to the Holy Rosary and said he recites fifteen mysteries daily. He acquired this devotion as Father Jorge Bergoglio in 1985 while attending a recitation of the Rosary being led by St. John Paul II. As he explained it, St. John Paul was on his knees, and his witness "struck me. I felt that this man, chosen to lead the Church, was following a path up to his Mother in the sky, a path set out on from childhood. . . . I understood the presence of Mary in the life of the Pope. That testimony did not get forgotten in an instant. From that time on I recite the fifteen mysteries of the Rosary every day."

In May 2014, Pope Francis advised the faithful that since May is the month devoted to Our Lady, it "is a fitting time to start the habit of a daily Rosary to earn graces that will help people overcome their problems in this troubling world."

Pope Francis fosters a devotion to Our Lady, Undoer of Knots, explaining that the knots represent the sins that separate us from God: "Mary, whose 'yes' opened the door for God to undo the knot of ancient disobedience, is the Mother who patiently and lovingly brings us unto God, so that he can untangle the knots of our soul by his fatherly mercy."

Now at this point there may occur a question in your minds that may puzzle or distract you. What about the times, you may ask, that will come after "our times"? What about that farther future of the world and of the Church? Will the Rosary still have its present privileged position in her teaching and treasury? Such a question, dear friends, is easily answered: it is simply idle to ask! The future, as Our Lord has told us, is hidden—not only from us but even from the angels of God (Mk 13:32; Acts 1:7).

But for all that, there is a looking forward that is not only proper but necessary, as again he has told us: "Watch and pray, for you know not the day nor the hour" (Mt 25:13). We indeed need to anticipate that moment that will surely come: the hour of our death. And so we pray: "Holy Mary, Mother of God, pray for us sinners now—and at the hour of our death." And if by that same hour "our times" will have ended too—whether in the catastrophe of total war, or in the decadence and paralysis of pseudo-peace, or in whatever other state the total world of human wills will have put us—we will at least have done all that we could do, and the rest is in the hands of God.

For the Mother of God—she who appeared at Fatima to at once reveal and veil the mysterious interaction of God's Providence and our prayer—she will have now commended that prayer of ours along with our soul to her Son.

And so, from that other world in the Church Triumphant or the Church Suffering, we will see the Church Militant enduring and striving, under Peter, until the end. Let this be the one answer to your question, then: as our present Holy Father has kept faith with his predecessors, so his successors will keep faith with him. The joys and sorrows of Jesus and Mary will remain to the end of time, and their glories will remain forever.

This ultimate glory is indeed before us now, revealed and hidden, in the Rosary. Regardless of what may come hereafter, our times are indeed "signed" — signed with that "great sign in heaven" that culminates the revelation of the Scriptures (Rev 12:1). This "woman clothed with the sun, with the moon beneath her feet, and crowned with stars" is Mary, Mother of the Church! She is the Woman who in the fullness of time mediated the formation of Christ's Body; and she mediates its completion now.

Christ, the New and Eternal Adam, is not alone (Gen 2:18–24). With him — at his cradle, at his Cross, at his heavenly throne — is she whom we hail, and repeatedly hail, as Mother of all the Living.

If in the Pauline teaching we read that "he who consecrates and those who are consecrated have the one and the same Father" (Heb 2:11), so in the Pauline teaching we know, with the growth of centuries in the tradition of this same one Catholic faith, that "he who consecrates and those who are consecrated" have the one and the same Mother!

As our beloved Pope Paul has reminded us, that same Blessed Mother has visited our poor world in these our days, and she has surely related to her Son in simple prayer that which she has seen: "They have no peace."*

May that prayer in Christ's good hour be granted, may all the children be gathered with their Father and their Mother, and may the entire family rejoice with the First-born Son — in the New Wine of his Peace.

---

* See *Christi Matri*, an encyclical of Pope Paul VI promulgated in 1966 to commemorate the fourth centenary of *Consueverunt Romani*, an apostolic letter of Pope St. Pius VI, who explained and fostered the traditional form of the Rosary.

THE
JOYFUL
MYSTERIES

THE FIRST
JOYFUL MYSTERY

✠

THE ANNUNCIATION

THE IMMACULATE
CONCEPTION

The Lord created me at the beginning of his work, the
first of his acts of old. Ages ago I was set up, at the first,
before the beginning of the world. (Prov 8:22–23)

OUR Rosary begins where Our Lady begins: in the mind and heart of the triune God. There from eternity she dwelt, until in time she received existence by his act of creation. Such a beginning is, of course, true of everything—from angels to atoms, ourselves included (cf. Eph 1:4).

But in this entire universe she is unique. She is the one creature who is simply perfect: the one who will correspond perfectly to his design of purest, fullest grace. Alone of all creatures, she is destined uniquely to enter into the mystery of God himself—in Trinity.

This predestination of Our Lady was primarily to provide the one creaturely factor in the mystery of "God with us"—the Word Incarnate, Our Lord Jesus Christ. She exists exclusively and totally in the mystery of God's Son—and hers. And the first facet of that mystery is that HE, Jesus, is, in his human nature, "grace" itself!

This is why we begin our Rosary right here in the very first instant of Our Lady's life: her being conceived in grace. Her conception thus ushers in the "new creation" (2 Cor 5:17), which immeasurably surpasses the "old creation," when God made the first man from dust in paradise. For grace now "more abounds" (cf. Rom 5:20), when God's promise of "the woman" and "her seed" (cf. Gen 3:15) begins its fulfillment—in Mary.

Yes, so personal and abiding is this "fullness of grace" promised and effected that Our Lady says to us at the beginning of her Rosary what she said at Lourdes: "I am the Immaculate Conception."

THE BIRTH OF MARY

... the virgin's name was Mary. (Lk 1:27)

IN her conception, the "immaculate" is truly a new beginning, for simply in her being conceived she is already "blessed among women." This befits her destiny to be the true "mother of all the living" (Gen 3:20): the second Eve, cooperating with the second Adam in the world's redemption from the original sin of the first Adam and Eve.

For all that, however, she had to have continuity not only with the total human race but also with that particular branch that stems from Abraham: God's chosen people. That continuity of descent is summarized in the first chapter of the first Gospel, where St. Matthew counts the "generations," and includes but four women: Tamar, Rahab, Ruth, and Bathsheba (Mt 1:3, 5, 6). Not Rachel, Deborah, Judith, and Esther, but a mixed lot of common humanity.

Thus, sometime in the last years of the last century of Israel's long expectation, out of the "remnant" of Abraham's seed and Jesse's root, there is born to a couple named Joachim and Anne a daughter named Mary.

We know next to nothing of Our Lady's birth, nor even the precise significance of her name. "Mary" is a name at once modest and majestic, Biblical and apocryphal, and the baby girl so named is at once a hidden rosebud in Galilee and a wondrous rainbow in heaven. For, according to the unbroken tradition of God's people, the Enemy from the beginning, the Serpent in Eden, will have his head crushed by a woman's heel (cf. Gen 3:15).

And now at last, as a newborn infant sleeps in her cradle, from under the coverlet a tiny foot stirs.

THE PRESENTATION
OF OUR LADY

In the holy tabernacle I ministered before him,
and I was established in Zion. (Sir 24:10)

SUMMARIZING the Old Testament and anticipating the New, the history of Our Lady proceeds
from Nazareth — the presumed site of her birth — to
Jerusalem, the Holy City. There, dominating the scene
as it does to this day, is Mount Moriah, the legendary
site of Adam's death and burial, and the historical site
of the Temple.

For almost a thousand years built and rebuilt, the
Temple was for Joachim and Anne the family hearth
where God dwells in the midst of his people. We may
imagine them there, standing at the foot of the stairs
leading up to the sanctuary. Climbing the stairs, all
alone with simplicity and dignity, is a little girl. At the
age of three, Mary is entering the Temple, to be presented to the Lord as his tiny handmaid — pending the
time when, like her ancestor Samuel, the Lord will
speak to her.

This scene is not in Sacred Scripture; it is a legend, meant to be symbolic. A symbol of what? Mary's
Immaculate Conception and birth are total gifts; in them,
as far as anyone can know, given the normal Providence
of God, she fulfills God's will by simply being.

But now, with the first budding of self-consciousness,
she sees her totally gifted self as totally his. Flowing
from her personal being as immaculate is her personal activity as totally sinless. Between these two
"moments" — the first, her infancy, and the second, the
rest of her life — her Presentation in the Temple is the
symbolic link.

THE ESPOUSAL OF OUR LADY

... a virgin betrothed to a man whose name was Joseph.
(Lk 1:27)

AT least a dozen years have passed in Mary's life, and now we see her in the fresh bloom of young womanhood. Inevitably, the scene is threaded with legend, each strand a bejeweled tribute to a beautiful girl on her betrothal day.

The event itself is factual: back in Nazareth of Galilee, a kinsman in the line of David named Joseph has won her hand. Some thirty years old, a carpenter by trade, sturdy and reserved, gentle and manly, Joseph is God's choice for Mary; the legends but embellish the simple truth.

Joining hands, they pledge their mutual troth. Henceforth until death, their joint lives will be ordered to but one thing: the oneness of God's will for them.

God's will for Mary and Joseph, beyond their engagement, is as yet not manifest to them. It calls for a total trust from them: trusting in God and in each other, waiting together for his further word to them. Mary trusts that her virginal love for God will remain in perpetuity, protected by her spouse. And Joseph trusts that his responsibility to God for her will be blessed beyond all his dreams.

Like the patriarch for whom he was named (and who was also a dreamer!), Joseph will indeed be blessed — blessed as the "fruitful bough" in Jacob's prophecy (cf. Gen 49:22). St. Joseph's legendary symbol is perfect: a flowering staff combines to perfection the strength and the sweetness that, with perfect complementarity, God has provided for Our Lady and for what awaits her.

NAZARETH

... a city of Galilee named Nazareth... (Lk 1:26)

NAZARETH is a little country town, so little it is not mentioned in the entire Old Testament. Yet for all that, it occupies as beautiful a site as anyone could wish. Perched on a kind of terrace amid verdant hills, it looks southward over the Plain of Esdraelon, the rich expanse of fields and flocks connecting the region around the Sea of Galilee with the coastal strip along the Mediterranean. Two mountains frame the panorama from left to right: to the east Mount Thabor, to the west Mount Carmel. What a setting for an event that would end the Old Testament and begin the New!

To think, however, that Nazareth is some idyllic place far removed from this poor fallen world is a mistake. Green smiling Galilee is no more immune to the ravages of original sin than is gray-grim Judea. The whole "circuit of the globe" — no place excepted — lies in darkness, as the Blessed Trinity looks down in pity on a spoiled creation. *

Even little hometown Nazareth has its meanness, its "nosiness," its obstinacy, its failure to comprehend the light (cf. Jn 1:5). "Can anything good come out of Nazareth?" What may have been a familiar taunt from its hill country neighbors is a matter of record (Jn 1:46). But likewise recorded is the rejoinder: "Come and see!"

Yes, Nazareth has a future! For see: here in this "back bench" lost along the highway of the world, in a little house tucked in among other little houses, there kneels in prayer "our tainted nature's solitary boast."

---

* See Louis J. Puhl, trans., *The Spiritual Exercises of St. Ignatius: A New Translation Based on Studies in the Language of the Autograph* (Newman Press, 1951), no. 102.

THE ANNUNCIATION
TO OUR LADY

[The angel Gabriel] came to her and said,
"Hail, full of grace." (Lk 1:28)

IT is springtime in Galilee. The equinox has just occurred, and now into this medley of day and night, of light and dark, with the day and the light now burgeoning, comes a word from heaven. St. Gabriel, the great angel who had come first to Daniel (Dan 9:21) and then to Zachary (Lk 1:19) to announce an ending to Israel's long wait, now comes to Nazareth, to that little house and chamber of a teenage girl. With a joy and courtesy straight from heaven, he bows before the Virgin Mary and addresses her as "full of grace."

"Full of grace." The Greek word *kekaritomene* means "someone favored — graced — to the ultimate degree." The angel uses this word in place of "Mary."

"Full of grace" is, in a sense, her very name! For it identifies her by something unique to her. She alone is "full of grace," for that is the reason for her unique prerogative and its positive meaning. The "Immaculata" is "spotless" — empty of sin because she is full of grace.

And the angel so addresses her now, for he has come to announce that "the Lord is with [her]" in a manner likewise unique and utterly transcendent. The Lord is already with her in the plenitude of grace from her conception, but now he is to be with her in the plenitude of his own humanity, which is grace incarnate. Her conception was his gift to her without her consent; his conception will be his gift to her only with her consent.

OUR LADY'S DISCERNMENT

"Do not be afraid, Mary....
You will conceive and bear a son...."

"How can this be?"

"The Holy Spirit will come upon you....
For with God nothing will be impossible."
(Lk 1:29–37)

OUR Lady's initial silence at the angel's greeting mirrors her soul: hailed "full of grace," she ponders in wonder the meaning of these words from heaven. Turned ever to God, she now turns to herself, since God himself has turned to her and is "with" her.

The angel reassures her — "Be not afraid, for perfect love casts out fear" (cf. 1 Jn 4:18). God is indeed with her, for now the message sent from heaven to her is this: she is to conceive a son to be named Jesus, who will be the Messiah, God's "Anointed One" and Israel's king.

Undaunted, undazzled at this prospect, she calmly voices the discernment that in that moment of silence her soul had made within her: how will this come to pass, since she has offered to God — and God has accepted — her virginity?

Mary's consecrated virginity, St. Gabriel replies in effect, far from being an impediment, is rather the very instrument of God's design! Her son Jesus will have but one Father — just as the Father and the mother will have but one Son. The Father will send his Holy Spirit to enfold her, so that the Child to be born will be indeed the all-holy One, the Anointed of God.

Thus does this Annunciation reveal for the first time the two great mysteries of our faith: the Trinity that is God, and the God-Man that is Christ — with both enshrined in the body and soul of Mary, ever-Virgin and Mother.

OUR LADY'S FIAT

Mary said, "Behold, I am the handmaid of the Lord,
let it be done to me according to your word." (Lk 1:38)

THE brief dialogue—a matter of minutes—between
Our Lady and the angel Gabriel, a dialogue of
words and silences, is now finished. Our Lady has all
she needs to know before she makes her decision; she
now knows what God intends to do and how he intends
to do it.

Will she consent to it? It is a matchless moment as
the angel, representing every created person but one
in the entire universe, awaits the one word from the
one created person before him through whom a whole
new universe will come to be: the universe of grace.
In a matchless manner St. Bernard has captured this
moment in one of his sermons on Our Lady.

And now, with a fullness of grace—in every sense
of that word—Mary responds: "be it done unto me
according to thy word."

Mary's *fiat* is the perfect creature's response to the
Creator's call, the perfect human "yes" corresponding
to the divine "yes." The angel had already said, "You
will conceive." But its actual happening depended on
her consent, which, in her fullness of grace, she could
not but give.

Here is the perfect instance of the simultaneous
mystery of divine grace and human freedom, of divine
operation and human cooperation, of divine revelation and human faith. Yes, human faith has no better
expression than this one little sentence spoken by Our
Lady. It shows the perfect blending of deliberation and
spontaneity, of solemnity and simplicity, of humility
and grace.

THE INCARNATION

. . . the Word became flesh and dwelt among us. (Jn 1:14)

AFTER Our Lady spoke her *fiat*, "the angel departed from her" (Lk 1:38). This quiet anticlimactic ending of St. Luke's exquisite narrative has had few if any portrayals in sacred art. But then, many of the portrayals of Our Lady in prayerful solitude evoke this moment in her life. Probably on her knees, her arms crossed upon her breast, her eyes closed, the Virgin Mary is all alone—with the Alone. "The mystery of the spheres conjoint: God focused to a point."

All the stupendous paradoxes of the Incarnation— the infinite and the finite, the endless litany of the opposite attributes of Creator and creature—are right here for the first time, and for eternity, set in place. And that place is the womb—and the soul—of the *Theotokos*, the "God-bearer."

Yes, Jesus was conceived in the soul of his Mother before being conceived in her body. For she first received the Word in her mind and will by faith, and then, by the mediation of her faith, the Word became flesh in her womb. Her motherhood was wholly conscious and willed; her soul as well as her body welcomed him, in that symbol of her entire personhood that is her heart.

From her heart had come the words *genoito moi—fiat mihi*—"be it done [to me]." By these words she effected her human cooperation, full and free, with the Spirit of God. For now, in her womb in the shadow of the Most High, the Word is made flesh.

THE MYSTERY OF
THE ANNUNCIATION

*Hail Mary, full of grace, the Lord is with
Thee. Blessed art thou among women, and
blessed is the fruit of thy womb, Jesus.*

THE First Joyful Mystery of the Rosary is the Hail
Mary in its origin. That origin goes back to God's
eternal decree of the Incarnation of his Son in time —
and therefore of the woman in whom the Incarnation
was to take place. Mary is that "blessed among women":
blessed in her birth, blessed in her childhood, blessed
in her adolescence and in her chosen spouse, and now
blessed in the supreme gift from heaven, the very Word
of God made Man, the fruit of her virginal womb.

The Mystery of the Annunciation gathers up all the
antecedent mysteries of her Immaculate Conception,
her Nativity, her Presentation, and her Espousal. Hidden
from us even in the pages of Sacred Scripture, they
become manifest in this Mystery of the Annunciation.

Yet this Mystery is but the beginning of the Rosary;
the mysteries that follow are still hidden — even, except
in broadest outline, from Mary herself.

As Our Lord told one of his disciples on another occasion,
"Greater things than these shall you see" (Jn 1:50).
Sufficient for us now is the faith and the humility of
Mary in this first Mystery of her Rosary. In all our
needs, present and future, we turn to her now, faithfully
and humbly, in petition:

*Holy Mary, Mother of God,
pray for us sinners, now and
at the hour of our death.
Amen.*

THE SECOND
JOYFUL MYSTERY

✠

THE VISITATION

OUR LADY'S JOURNEY

... Mary arose and went with haste into the
hill country, to a city of Judah ... (Lk 1:39)

OUR Lady's silent prayer of welcome to her Son
may well have been the first "holy hour": the first
hour of his existence in time was thus shared exclusively with his Mother. What hour was it on the clock?
We do not know, nor will we until we enter eternity;
for only then will we really know that any and every
hour could have been a holy hour, living in the presence
of Jesus and Mary.

Let us say for now that it was night, yet at that late
hour of the night when the eastern sky is aglow with
the morning star. Then, like a bridegroom leaving his
chamber, like a giant rejoicing to run his course (cf. Ps
18/19:5), the Word moves his Mother to carry him on
a journey: the "Good News" must be spread. And so,
"she arose and went with haste."

The details of the sixty-mile journey across the budding Holy Land are omitted by St. Luke. What holds
his attention is that it was quickly done. Yes, the jubi-
lant energy of this young womanhood, matching the
energy of its tiny treasure, for it is he, "the beloved,
leaping upon the mountains, bounding over the hills"
(Cant 2:8).

The unborn Christ is intent upon his task. For what
was written of him in the head of the book must be fulfilled: "... a body thou hast prepared for me.... Then
I said: Behold, I have come to do thy will, O God"
(Heb 10:5, 7).

OUR LADY'S GREETING

. . . she entered the house of Zechariah
and greeted Elizabeth. (Lk 1:40)

ST. Luke in his narrative of the Annunciation tells us that Our Lady spoke twice to the angel Gabriel, once in question and once in response; and we have the very words she spoke. In his narrative of the Visitation, he tells us that again she spoke twice, this time to her cousin Elizabeth, for whose sake she had made this hasty journey.

Her first speaking is immediately on her arrival in the house; she "greeted Elizabeth." Her greeting is more than her embrace of her cousin — the womanly gesture which nearly all the artists of this scene have depicted. No, she also spoke her greeting, for in the following verse we are told that Elizabeth "heard the greeting of Mary."

But what words there were, St. Luke does not say. Perhaps it was but one word, the word with which the angel had greeted her: *Chaire* (or in Latin, *Ave*).

Mary is thus the sender as well as the receiver of the reality called "rejoicing" (for that is what *Ave* means in English: "Hail" or "Rejoice"). She is indeed the mediatrix — and in that sense the cause — of all our joy!

Her word of greeting to Elizabeth heralds the "Good News" that God is with us, in the Person of his unborn Son. Yes, this is God's will: that his Son be brought, in his newly created Body, to all mankind, beginning with his people Israel, represented by this elderly couple, Zechariah and Elizabeth, and their unborn son.

JOHN'S SANCTIFICATION

... when Elizabeth heard the greeting of Mary,
the baby leaped in her womb, and Elizabeth
was filled with the Holy Spirit. (Lk 1:41)

NO sooner had the aged Elizabeth been embraced by young Mary and heard her "Ave!" greeting than a rapturous experience ensued. Six months pregnant, Elizabeth felt a sudden movement of her child. Whether or not she was aware of the natural phenomenon called "quickening" is irrelevant; she herself at this moment is aware of something supernatural: the presence of the Holy Spirit.

With this spontaneous movement of word and gesture on the part of Our Lady and its equally spontaneous sequel on the part of Elizabeth and her unborn child, at this first moment of their meeting, we have the essential purpose of Our Lady's Visitation fulfilled.

Using Mary's word of greeting and accompanying gesture as his instrument, the Holy Spirit descends on Elizabeth and her child. His action proceeds from child to mother: the first effect of Our Lady's cooperating action is the baby's leaping.

What meaning does this little incident, so exquisitely portrayed, have for us? The Church's tradition sees in this "quickening" of the unborn John his baptism! Yes, this is the first "sacrament" of the New Testament: the word and gesture placed by the unborn Christ's Mother acting as his handmaid signify and cause a wholly new life in one whose natural life had already begun.

And the sanctifying grace in the soul of John "the Baptized" reverberates in his body—and in the soul of his mother. Thus both son and mother are sanctified by the Holy Spirit proceeding from another Son acting through his Mother.

ELIZABETH'S BLESSING

... [Elizabeth] exclaimed... "Blessed are you among
women, and blessed is the fruit of your womb!"
... And blessed is she who believed that there
would be a fulfillment of what was spoken
to her by the Lord. (Lk 1:42–45)

THE Holy Spirit's presence in Elizabeth quickens in her the gift of prophecy, as "with a loud voice" she proclaims the glory of her little cousin Mary, Virgin and Mother. And so, if the Hail Mary's beginning came from heaven, conveyed by an angel, its ending comes from earth, conveyed by a woman. Elizabeth speaks for all her sisters, all the daughters of Eve: here at last is the Woman blessed among all women in her virginity, and even more blessed in her motherhood—in the fruit of her womb.

Indeed, her motherhood is the culminating title of her blessedness: the Lord—Yahweh himself—is her Son! And whence came this doubly compounded blessedness? From her faith! The word spoken to her by God through his angel she received in her soul and body—in her entire person; and by her receiving it, it will be fulfilled!

The triple blessing by Elizabeth is the first recognition of Our Lady's blessedness, already present in her, first by the power of God and secondly by her cooperation with that power in her virginity, her motherhood, and her faith.

The Church's faith, modelled on Mary's faith, repeats her praises, using Elizabeth's words. All our prayers to her, beginning with the Church's own prayer to "Holy Mary," following and completing the "Hail Mary" of Gabriel and Elizabeth, are but echoes of those few words, angelically and humanly spoken but divinely inspired, which first rang out across the Holy Land in springtime splendor.

THE MAGNIFICAT—1

*My soul magnifies the Lord, and my spirit rejoices
in God my Savior.... For behold, henceforth all
generations will call me blessed;... He who is
mighty has done great things for me.... His mercy
is on those who fear him.... (Lk 1:46–50)*

AFTER Our Lady greeted her cousin, most probably
with the one word "Ave!" spoken by Gabriel to herself, and after Elizabeth responded with her prophetic
threefold blessing, there comes from the heart and lips
of Mary the first and greatest of all the songs recorded
in the New Testament: the *Magnificat*. It is the Gospel canticle *par excellence*: the one fullest statement by
Our Lady herself of what the Incarnation of the Son
of God—the event for the effecting of which she was
created—means to her, and through her, to us all.

She stands there before Elizabeth—and us—in the
glow of eventide, and hymns the magnificence of God
and the lowliness of his handmaid. True, she echoes
the canticle of Anna, her mother's patron saint (cf.
1 Sam 2:1–10), but now how immeasurably more magnificent is God—her savior, her "Jesus," in his mercy,
and how immeasurably more blessed is she in her truth.

Straight from the Spouse of the Holy Spirit, it is
the perfect statement of the "Good News," in a perfect
setting of its core truth and beauty: God's greatness
is made greater—it is magnified!—by his handmaid's
humility.

Her exaltation in this truth of the Creator and the
creature only makes it more true! Here is her only joy,
her only grace: she can actually give to God—and
have accepted by him—her nothingness. For out of
this nothingness has come his mercy—"from generation to generation"—the Mercy Incarnate now cradled
under her heart.

THE MAGNIFICAT—2

. . . He has scattered the proud in the imagination
of their hearts . . . He has filled the hungry with
good things. . . . He has helped his servant Israel,
in remembrance of his mercy. . . (Lk 1:51–55)

IN her canticle, Our Lady turns herself to God, and
from God to herself—and to all the generations that
will henceforth call her "blessed." The remembered
solitude of the Annunciation has turned to the busy
multitude, which the Visitation now brings into her
view. This too must be addressed in her song of praise,
for it is the world—the real world, the workaday world
of fallen humanity—into which her God and Savior
has come.

Just as she anticipated by her *fiat* the *ecce venio* spoken
by her unborn Son, so too she now anticipates, in the
second part of her *Magnificat*, the Beatitudes.

In the Sermon on the Mount, we will have at last the
New Law of the Kingdom: where every injustice stemming from the pride of the original sin will be reversed,
and where every expectation arising from the goodness
of the original creation will be fulfilled.

The Messianic reign of justice and love will banish
all sin and disorder, and the beatitude of heaven will
have its beginning on earth! For such is God's mercy as
promised to his Prophets, and abiding forever.

And who could more fittingly prophesy this definitive
coming of the Kingdom than she who, even now in total
sinlessness, carries in her body the King!

THE BIRTH OF
ST. JOHN THE BAPTIST

*[Elizabeth] gave birth to a son. And her neighbors
and kinsfolk ... rejoiced with her.... And all laid
up [these things] in their hearts, saying, "What
then will this child be?" For the hand of the
Lord was with him. (Lk 1:57–58, 66)*

S T. Luke tells us that Our Lady stayed with her
cousin for "about three months" and then returned
to her home in Nazareth (Lk 1:56). Although he puts
this in his narrative immediately after the *Magnificat*,
and therefore before the birth of Elizabeth's son, it
would seem more likely that Mary extended her Visitation to include that event — as any natural consideration
would suppose, and as the original date for the liturgical
celebration (July 2) would suggest.

We may therefore contemplate Our Lady's contemplation of the newborn child, and find in him what
she must have found: the marvelous linkage in God's
plan of the Old Testament with the New. He is the
offspring of an aged couple, heralded in God's temple
by an angel and sanctified in his mother's womb by
Mary's Visitation.

Yes, John the Baptist would someday be identified
by Jesus as "the greatest man born of woman," and
yet "he who is least in the kingdom of heaven is greater
than he" (Mt 11:11). So indeed, the last and greatest
of the prophets would himself yield to the younger
Man who came after him and yet was before him —
who must, therefore, increase while he, John, would
decrease (cf. Jn 3:30).

Did Our Lady ever see John in his adulthood? We
do not know. In any case, she sees him now in his cradle; she sees the first fulfillment of her role as "blessed
handmaid." Is she not here the little servant of the
first-born servant of the Lord?

THE BENEDICTUS

*Blessed be the Lord God of Israel, for he has visited
and redeemed his people . . . as he spoke by the mouth
of his holy prophets of old . . . to perform the mercy
promised to our fathers, and to remember his holy
covenant. And you, child, . . . will go before the Lord
to prepare his ways, . . . when the day star shall
dawn upon us from on high. . . . (Lk 1:68–79)*

IN the opening scene of St. Luke's Gospel, Zechariah
responded with disbelief to the angel's announce-
ment of the coming birth of John the Baptist, and for
his disbelief he was struck dumb (Lk 1:20).

Now, immediately following the birth of his little
son, "his mouth was opened and his tongue loosed, and
he spoke, blessing God" (Lk 1:64). This blessing took
the form of a canticle, the second of the four that St.
Luke will record in his Infancy Gospel. The *Benedictus* is longer, more ornate, more "priestly" than the
Magnificat, but the two make a perfect match — as the
Church recites them respectively in her morning and
her evening prayers every day of the year. Zechariah
echoes his wife's blessing of Mary, for he too sings of
the Visitation of God's redeeming love for his people
Israel, from Abraham to David to this newborn John.

This child, when he finds his voice, will indeed be
the prophet of the Most High, going before the Lord
to prepare his way — as the day star heralds the sun.
And as for Our Lady silently exulting in this canticle
of high summertime, she is reminded that the evening
star and the morning star are the same one light on high,
reflecting the same one setting and rising sun!

This sun is her Son, her Savior — who is the "peace"
with which word the canticle closes (cf. Mic 5:5, Vulgate). And the "path of peace" is her path, back to Nazareth, where she will await — as she has always awaited —
the disposition of God's Providence.

THE ANNUNCIATION
TO ST. JOSEPH

*... an angel of the Lord appeared to him in a dream,
saying, "Joseph, son of David, do not fear to take
Mary your wife.... She will bear a son, and you
shall call his name Jesus." (Mt 1:20–21)*

SOMETIME after Our Lady's return to Nazareth, there occurred what we can call the "second Annunciation," when the coming of Our Lord to earth was for a second time announced from heaven. St. Matthew's Infancy Gospel complements St. Luke's, and fittingly so, for if St. Luke writes his account from the perspective of Our Lady (cf. Lk 2:19, 51), St. Matthew gives us essentially the same story from St. Joseph's point of view.

It is a fitting complementarity for, as both sacred authors tell us, St. Joseph and Our Lady were a married couple, and so the story of the origin and childhood of Jesus is part — indeed the supreme part — of their common property.

To begin with, St. Matthew had already told us that Our Lord's Messianic title "Son of David" derives from Joseph's lineage: before God and man, Jesus is the "Son of Joseph" (cf. Lk 3:24; Jn 1:45). This is because Mary, Jesus's mother, is Joseph's lawful wife.

Now, it is precisely to reassure Joseph of this fact that this Annunciation takes place. Note two significant details. First, its delay: a touch of mystery and a trial, a shadow that would only enhance the light of the angel's disclosure. And secondly, its occurring in a dream: calling for no spoken response on Joseph's part. He is simply to do what God has decreed: he is now to become the earthly shadow of the eternal Father!

We can but contemplate — with Mary — his noble humility, his eloquent silence. St. Joseph is indeed the "just man" (Mt 1:19): the perfect husband and father.

THE MYSTERY OF
THE VISITATION

*Hail Mary, full of grace, the Lord is with
thee, blessed art thou among women, and
blessed is the fruit of thy womb, Jesus.*

THE Second Joyful Mystery of the Rosary is the
perfect sequel to the First Mystery, which is essentially the Mystery of the Incarnation itself. The Son of
God's becoming the Son of Mary is a reality that must
be revealed — its revelation is our faith!

The Visitation is that revelation's beginning: its
springtime budding! By the spontaneity, the diligence,
the sweetness of her actions and words, Our Lady
mediates the revelation and its grace. And the result is
a sanctification, a wonder, and a joy that will forever
after characterize the Gospel of Jesus Christ.

The blessed saints who accompany Our Lady in this
Mystery we must also note. Zechariah and Elizabeth
are worthy successors of Joachim and Anne: "righteous before God and blameless" (Lk 1:6), they exemplify the "remnant," the last best hope of old Israel.
The marvelous birth of their son John is enshrined
between two canticles and is celebrated as a solemnity
in the Church.

Paired with him in the sacred liturgy is the one who,
of all saints and angels, is closest to Our Lady and her
Son: St. Joseph. With him we will continue in our Joyful
Mysteries, for they are the memories and mysteries of
a Family of which he is the head.

*Holy Mary, Mother of God,
pray for us sinners, now and
at the hour of our death.
Amen.*

THE THIRD
JOYFUL MYSTERY

✠

THE NATIVITY

THE "FULLNESS OF TIME"

... when the time had fully come, God sent
his Son, born of a woman... (Gal 4:4)

WHAT does St. Paul mean when he says that "in the fullness of time" God sent his Son to be born of a woman? It cannot mean that time had reached its end, for it is now two thousand years after that "ending." Nor can it mean that time has simply "stopped," for time is by definition the measure of motion.

It can only mean, then, that at that given moment, when the Son entered into time by his becoming man, the quality of time was essentially changed. For then—and forever thereafter—time was, as it were, caught up into the eternal, just as the human was caught up into the divine when the Word was made flesh. Neither absorbed by eternity nor absorbing it in turn, time now has, in its finiteness, an infinite worth.

This infinity began with the Incarnation, but the manifestation of this infinity would begin only gradually. Indeed, it would not completely manifest until time itself would end, as we know it will, when the same Son of God will come again in his glory. Then will come that "fullness of time" in which, as St. Paul elsewhere says, all things will be restored in Christ, both in heaven and on earth (cf. Eph 1:10).

But for now, in our Rosary prayer accompanying Our Lady, we look back to that "first" fullness of time—and find that it is indeed now, in our present time, that it is taking place "all over again."

BETHLEHEM

*...Joseph ... went up from Galilee, from the city
of Nazareth, to Judea, to the city of David,
which is called Bethlehem... (Lk 2:4)*

THE "fullness of time," as decreed by his counsel
from eternity, was indeed in God's possession, as
was also a "fullness of space"; for was not his the entire
earth and all the boundless stretches of the universe
beyond? But both these "fullnesses" were as yet not
revealed, so as to be clearly recognized by men.

What was universally recognized was that human
"fullness" of time and space called the Roman Empire.
In terms of time, it was already "the Eternal City," and
in terms of space, its rule was coextensive with the *orbis
terrarum*: the lands circling the Mediterranean, and in
effect the "circle of the earth" itself.

Now, in God's decree, his "fullness" would begin its
manifestation by using the seeming fullness of creaturely Rome as the signal for his coming.

And so the master of Rome, Octavian Caesar Augus-
tus, sent forth his decree that a census of the whole
world should be made. Accordingly, Joseph with Mary
left Galilean Nazareth for the distant city of his family's
origin, Bethlehem of Judah. It is now winter, and the
overcrowded little town has no room left for them. It is
cold and dark when Joseph finally finds an unoccupied
shelter for his wife, weary from the journey and nearing
the completion of her pregnancy.

The cave-like stable is quiet but for the soft lowing
of animals and the rustling of straw. Joseph fits out a
rustic feedbox, and beside it kneels Mary, all lost in
poverty — and prayer.

THE BIRTH OF OUR LORD

... [Mary] gave birth to her first-born Son... (Lk 2:7)

THE simplicity of St. Luke's account of the birth of Our Lord is a masterpiece, even as compared with the whole of his Infancy Gospel. What is in fact the very center of that little Gospel, as exactly reflected in the sacred liturgy of the Christmas cycle centering on the Midnight Mass of Christmas, is the unique and indivisible moment of Jesus's birth.

True, the moment of the Incarnation is nine months past — "Emmanuel" is already here! Yet it is the moment of his birth that brings to us the primordial mystery of his Person: the mystery of his being the eternal and only-begotten Son. Every subsequent mystery of his life — including the Paschal Mystery itself — presupposes this Mystery of his birth, which identifies his very Person as the One "begotten not made," or, more simply put, as the "One who is Born."

St. Luke's simplicity of words cannot match the simplicity of the ineffable event itself. We know by the defined faith of the Church what the sacred text itself suggests: that the birth of Jesus in his humanity was a miraculous birth.

Led into all truth by the Holy Spirit (cf. Jn 16:13), the ancient Church affirmed again and again Our Lady's perpetual virginity. She is "ever Virgin," and so the manner of Jesus's birth is in total harmony with the manner of his conception — and in perfect analogy with his birth in his divinity. From his Mother in time as from his Father in eternity, Our Lord is virginally born.

OUR LADY'S MOTHERHOOD

...she wrapped him in swaddling clothes,
and laid him in a manger... (Lk 2:7)

OUR Lord's birth in Bethlehem on that first Christmas night was the perfect human counterpart to his birth of the Father "before all ages." Its very simplicity was most fittingly divine. Yet the divine, as we learn from its revelation in the Old Testament, is not only perfectly transcendent; it is also perfectly immanent.

God is at once the most immense and the most intimate: infinitely beyond all his creatures, and inconceivably near—nearer to them than they are to themselves. And now in his human birth both aspects intertwine, and supremely so in the heart of that one creature of his who gave him his humanity. See her now as she enfolds him to her breast: this tiny swaddled bundle of infinity.

The contemplation of Jesus by Mary his Mother is in itself a single object of contemplation by all the rest of us.* Beginning with St. Joseph there beside her on his knees, all mankind beholds but one indivisible reality. "Round yon virgin mother and child": a young mother beholding "her first-born Son," and a newborn baby beholding his mother.

She has eyes only for him as she takes him in her arms to warm him, to nurse him, to coo to him, to make him at home. Years later, as a crowd gathered around the young Rabbi from Nazareth to contemplate his parables and miracles, a nameless woman in its midst cried out to him, "Blessed is the womb that bore you, and the breasts that nursed you!" (Lk 11:27).

Yes, "blessed!"

---

* See Puhl, *The Spiritual Exercises of St. Ignatius*, no. 114.

THE "GLORIA"

*... an angel of the Lord appeared to [the
shepherds] ... and ... said to them, "Be not
afraid; for behold I bring you good news of a great
joy...." And suddenly there was with the angel a
multitude of the heavenly host praising God and
saying, "Glory to God in the highest, and peace on
earth to men of good will." (Lk 2:9–10, 13–14)*

THE mystery of the Incarnation is the essential but
not the exclusive object of the Christmas celebration. We celebrate this central mystery of our faith—the
union of divinity and humanity in the one Person of
our Lord Jesus Christ—in the context of the broader
mystery of Creation itself.

The Infant Jesus is not only fully human (indeed, he
is Everyman!); he is also "the first-born of all creation"
(Col 1:15). All God's creatures, therefore, both those
above man and those below him, have their place in the
Christmas scene. The traditional crèche, dating back to
St. Francis of Assisi, would not be complete without the
animals—an ox, a donkey, and some sheep—and at least
one angel. In the original Gospel narrative, St. Luke
suggests the presence of the animals, but he is explicit
about the angels; "a multitude of the heavenly host" is
both seen and heard.

Following Our Lady's and St. Joseph's adoration of
Jesus comes the act of adoration by his superhuman
creatures, the pure spirits who in their myriad numbers
surround God's throne and mediate to the universe his
rule. Their appearance on this Christmas night fulfills
the dream of Jacob's Ladder: ascending angels offer
"glory to God in the highest," while descending angels
proclaim "peace on earth to men of good will."

St. Luke's third recorded canticle, this song of the
angels, fills the cosmos; yet see how intimately personal
it is to each one of us! For was not my own guardian
angel also there that night?

THE SHEPHERDS

. . . [the shepherds] went with haste, and found Mary
and Joseph, and the baby lying in a manger. And
the shepherds returned, glorifying and praising God
for all they had heard and seen. . . (Lk 2:16–20)

SEEING and hearing the angels that Christmas night
were shepherds, simple folk of the countryside, tending their flock. They were the first ones to receive from
heaven "the good news of great joy" — the first ones
to hear the words "Savior" and "Christ" and "Lord"
applied as a present fact to Someone now on earth.

The shepherds are invited to see him for themselves;
they can go now just as they are, for he is a tiny baby
in a manger nearby. So, hurrying across the fields, they
find the Holy Family and offer them welcome, the
belated welcome of their little town.

How many shepherds were there? And how old and
how young were they? Unnumbered and nameless, they
are nevertheless the heirs of David, who tended sheep
in these same fields, and the forebears of Peter and the
other Apostles, who someday would stand in for the
Good Shepherd himself, tending and feeding his one
flock across a whole wide world.

But tonight, all that is either in the past or in the
future. Right now, we have but to "see this thing which
has happened, which the Lord has made known to us"
(Lk 2:15). Our seeing may be helped by hundreds of
master paintings and thousands of Christmas cards. And
accompanying our seeing may be music, which we can
make on flute or drum, to echo the angels. In any case,
we can hum or whisper words to add to the album Our
Lady is keeping in her heart (cf. Lk 2:19).

THE HOLY NAME

... at the end of eight days, when he was circumcised,
he was called Jesus, the name given by the angel
before he was conceived in the womb. (Lk 2:21)

AFTER eight days, in accordance with the Law of
Moses, the Infant Jesus is circumcised, and is thus
initiated into the Covenant that God had first made with
Abraham. It is a covenant sealed in blood, and now for
the first time, with the first drops shed of this Baby's
blood, God makes his promise of a New and Eternal
Covenant to all mankind.

This must be what St. Joseph is thinking of as he
holds in his hands his tiny Son. For he remembers what
the angel had told him six months ago in Nazareth, that
"this child will save his people from their sins" (Mt 1:21).
In accordance with that message from heaven, he now
gives to this Child the Name "Jesus."

"Jesus" is a Name at once earthly and heavenly,
human and divine. It occurs occasionally in the Old
Testament; after all, it is the same word as "Joshua," the
name of Moses's successor, who led the Israelites into
the Promised Land.

But this name also comes from heaven — a "new
name" uniquely his (cf. Rev 2:17). It means "Yahweh
saves" or simply "Savior," and so it is, in one little word,
the total reality of this one Person, Christ the Lord, true
God and true Man.

Someday, when all will have been fulfilled and the
New Covenant is completed, this week-old Baby in his
parents' arms will appear in the clouds of heaven, and
in heaven, on earth, and under the earth, every knee
will bend at the sound of his Holy Name.

THE STAR OF BETHLEHEM

When [the wise men] saw the star, they rejoiced
exceedingly with great joy... (Mt 2:10)

SOMETIME after the Christmas happenings narrated by St. Luke, there occurs an event of singular mystery, which rounds out the Holy Family's memories of the birth of Jesus. One night, out of seeming nowhere, a gorgeous panoply appears at the doorway of their little abode. The simple shepherds had come from the nearby fields at the behest of an angel. Now there come Magi — "wise men" — from a great distance, guided to this place by a star!

They had first gone to Jerusalem, seeking the whereabouts of a newborn king, and they were told that an ancient prophecy had named Bethlehem as his birthplace. But what confirmed the prophecy was a star! For there it was, the same star they had first seen in the East, "over the place where the child was" (Mt 2:9). And seeing the star, "they rejoiced exceedingly with great joy."

Why all this "exceeding great joy"? Because what had once been reserved to God's people alone — the People of the Covenant — has now been opened to all peoples everywhere. Privileged Israel has learned from angels that its promised Messiah has come. Now the pagans will learn of his coming by a sign once dimly foreseen by one of their sages named Balaam (cf. Num 24:17): the silent witness of a distant star.

If someday the King of the universe will be acclaimed by the rending of rocks underfoot (cf. Mt 27:51, Lk 19:40), this night he is acclaimed by light from the far reaches of space. The cosmos itself belongs to him whom wise men adore.

THE MAGI

... going into the house they saw the child
with Mary his Mother, and they fell down
and worshipped him. (Mt 2:11)

A TRADITION stemming from St. Joseph (which is the probable source of St. Matthew's narrative) notes but one detail of what the Magi saw upon their entering where the Christmas star had directed them: "they found the Child with Mary his Mother." It is from St. Joseph, then, that we trace the wisdom of what two thousand years of Christmas art have shown us: the Madonna and Child.

Here is wisdom, for here is the truth of the Incarnation, the central mystery of our faith, that God is indeed with us! He who dwells beyond the stars in light inaccessible (cf. 1 Tim 6:16) is now with us, because he has a mother—whom he has made the very lamp of his manifestation, his "morning star" (cf. Rev 2:28), his Epiphany!

As wisdom is here, so too is beauty—the glorious beauty of nature and art combined in one exquisite scene. The Magi are now kneeling before the little Child presented to them by his Mother. They kiss his tiny toes and offer him the treasures they have brought from their homelands: the most precious things they can think of as symbols of his glory and their praise. Gold, frankincense, and myrrh—the joint products of God's creation and man's workmanship—they offer to their King and Savior.

See how the three jeweled coffers sparkle in the light that fills that little house! See how the hearts of all present are aglow—in the light and warmth of this finale of the Christmas mystery!

THE MYSTERY OF
THE NATIVITY

*Hail Mary, full of grace, the Lord is with
thee, blessed art thou among women, and
blessed is the fruit of thy womb, Jesus.*

OF all the mysteries of Our Lord's life, the one that
has most endeared itself to the Christian people is
undoubtedly the mystery of his birth. Just as from all
eternity he has been "the One who is Born," so too in
time he will always be the same: the One whose birth
signals a new age that will never end, being ever new!

He will always be the Newborn One, whose birthday
will always be the favorite day of the year; the day that
will forever be special to the family and children, to the
fireside and home.

If this is so for us, how much more so must it be for
Our Lady! If every mother keeps closest to her heart the
memory of her child in the very moment of his birth,
what must be Mary's memory of the moment when
for the very first time Jesus was seen — and seen by her?

Others enter soon into her vision: St. Joseph, the
angels, the shepherds, the Magi — and lastly, us. To all
of us she shows her little Son: the One so long awaited
by his family, so made welcome to his home, so warm
and warming by the pulsing fire of his tiny Heart.

*Holy Mary, Mother of God,
pray for us sinners, now and
at the hour of our death.
Amen.*

THE FOURTH
JOYFUL MYSTERY

✠

THE PRESENTATION
OF OUR LORD
IN THE TEMPLE

THE TEMPLE

*As he came out of the Temple, one of his disciples
said to him, "Look, Master, what wonderful stones
and what wonderful buildings!" (Mk 13:1)*

THUS far in the life of the Incarnate Son of God,
two places in the Holy Land have been especially
blessed by his presence: Nazareth in Galilee, where he
was conceived, and Bethlehem in Judea, where he was
born.

Now for the first time he will enter the city where
in due course he will die—and rise again: Jerusalem.
Again, in due course, his sepulcher will be the "holy of
holies" in that Holy City.

But now, as for the past thousand years since David
made Jerusalem his capital, the "holy of holies"—the
actual dwelling place of Yahweh amidst his people—is
in the Temple built by David's son Solomon and later
rebuilt following the Babylonian Exile.

Here will be the focal point of Our Lord's earthly life.
Up to the very day of his death, the Temple will be for
Jesus, as it was (and still is) for his people according to
the flesh, the one and only sanctuary of Israel's worship
and the one and only tabernacle of God's glory on earth.

Imagine, then, the feelings of Our Lady and St.
Joseph as they enter the Holy City with their month-old
Baby. They approach Jerusalem from the south; on their
right is Mount Olivet and on their left Mount Sion. In
between is Mount Moriah, the Temple Mount, with the
Valley of Kedron skirting its ramparts. Going up this
valley, they continue their ascent to the Temple itself
until they reach its Eastern Gate, now ablaze in the
splendor of the morning sun.

THE PRESENTATION
OF OUR LORD

... when the time came for their purification they
brought him up to Jerusalem to present him to the
Lord ... and to offer a sacrifice according to what
is said in the law of the Lord ... (Lk 2:22, 24)

THE Holy Family now enters the Temple precincts.
Our Lady carrying Jesus, St. Joseph carrying two
young pigeons. The Law of Moses had prescribed that
the mother of a son must come to the priest to be purified of her childbirth and to present her son, on the
fortieth day of his life, to the Lord. The little boy child
would then be "redeemed," bought back from God by
the offering of two little animals in his place. If the family could afford it, the animals to be sacrificed should
be a lamb and a dove; if they could not afford it, two
doves would suffice (cf. Lev 12:4–8).

And so, across the great courtyard they come, looking for a priest to perform the ceremony there at the
entrance of the great Temple itself.

Thus is fulfilled what the last of the prophets of the
Old Testament canon had foretold: the Lord of Hosts
will himself appear in his Temple, to purify the priests
and vindicate his people (Mal 3:1–5).

But see how this prophecy is fulfilled! The mother
to be purified is the Immaculata! And the child to be
redeemed is the Redeemer!

The purity and poverty of this little family is offered
to God in this first act of total humility. Our Lord has
come to accomplish the sacrifice that will transcend this
Temple — "the clean oblation ... from the rising to the
setting of the sun" (Mal 1:11). Yes, he has indeed come!
And he now begins the Liturgy of his Eucharist with
this celebration of his Offertory.

THE NUNC DIMITTIS

Lord, now lettest thou thy servant depart in peace,
according to thy word. . . . For mine eyes have seen
thy salvation . . . a light for revelation to the Gentiles,
and for glory to thy people Israel. (Lk 2:25–32)

FOR all its humility, this first visit of Jesus to his Temple does not pass unnoticed. An old man named Simeon had been praying for years that he might not die before he had seen the promised Messiah.

Moved by the Holy Spirit, he comes to the Temple this morning, and there he recognizes in the arms of this young mother the goal of his quest. This baby boy, tucked in his blanket and sleeping on his Mother's breast, is he! — the Anointed One of God, for whom this whole great Temple had been built, and in whom the thousand-year wait of Israel now comes to rest.

Simeon takes the Baby into his own arms, as Mary and Joseph stand by in wonder. Then with an ancient voice vibrant with joy, he sings a canticle, the last and most poignant of the Gospel's songs.

With the cadence of the Psalms, which all his life long he had sung, old Simeon gathers up in one inspired sentence the expectations of all mankind. Over all the nations of the earth a light has risen: the *Lumen Gentium* that will dispel all darkness. And for God's own people, his Church, with its Old Covenant now completed and its New Covenant now beginning, there is "Glory" — the glory of the Only-Begotten, full of grace and truth (cf. Jn 1:14).

This old man's song is as new as a baby's: it ends the Church's prayer each night by thanking God for his promise of perpetual light.

SIMEON'S PROPHECY

*... and Simeon said to Mary his mother, "Behold,
this Child is set for the fall and rising of many
in Israel, ... and a sword will pierce through
thy own soul also ..." (Lk 2:34–35)*

AFTER Simeon finishes his canticle of joy, he turns
to the Baby's parents and blesses them. Then, still
holding Jesus, he speaks to Mary. His eyes agleam with
the Holy Spirit, his words are still poetic with prophecy.

He bids her to see what he now sees: "this Child is
set for the fall and for the rising of many ..." The "rising"—yes! "Light" and "glory" he has already sung;
but before the "rising" there must be a "fall." The Holy
Spirit must have told Simeon—how otherwise could he
have known?—that already he had come unto his own,
and his own had received him not (cf. Jn 1:14).

That first "fall" was to be but the beginning of many
more. As long as he lives, he will divide people: some for
and some against. No one will ever be the same again,
as though he had never come.

Yes, he is "set for a sign that will be spoken against."
He will be opposed, contradicted, crossed. Does Simeon
see in prophecy the Sign of the Cross? If he does, he
calls it a "sword"—a sword that will pierce the soul of
this Child's Mother.

See now Our Lady, as in silent wonder she takes
back her Child. He has been offered to God. Is he still
hers? Now begins the "revelation of many hearts"—the
sword has opened them.

THE HOLY FAMILY

"And the child grew and became strong,
filled with wisdom; and the favor of
God was upon him." (Lk 2:40)

THE narrative of Our Lord's Presentation ends with an invitation to some silent contemplation. St. Luke bids us see Jesus as he grows.

Looking at him through Mary's eyes, we see her Baby taking his first steps, leaving infancy to become a little boy, a "toddler." We must see him now through Joseph's eyes as well. Mothers may want their babies always such — and after Simeon's prophecy, Our Lady's natural instinct may have been reinforced: she must protect him against a haunting fear. But fathers see their sons as junior partners. "Joseph and Son" — he may already be seeing the sign over his carpenter shop.

Modelling our contemplation on theirs, we Christians have created a two-thousand-year tradition of sacred art. With what a variety of light and shadow, or piquant detail and elusive symbol, have we surrounded this "earthly trinity" through those fleeting but eternal years of Jesus' childhood.

But the composition is not complete without the heavenly Trinity being also seen. True, there is no real revelation of this supreme mystery until Our Lord's baptism, but nevertheless both the Father and the Holy Spirit are already here in the Infancy Gospel. St. Luke tells us that "the favor of God was upon him." "God" is Yahweh, the one true Father of Jesus, while the "favor" — or "grace" — is the very Person of the Holy Spirit.

So this little "toddler" is One with Them, just as he is One with Mary and Joseph.

THE FLIGHT INTO EGYPT

... an angel of the Lord appeared to Joseph in a dream and said, "Rise, take the Child and his mother, and flee to Egypt."... And he rose and took the Child and his mother by night, and departed to Egypt. (Mt 2:13–14)

THE "light of the Gentiles" sung by Simeon is essentially the same as the light of the star seen by the Magi. That same one light is now aglow in the body and soul of one little Boy, at once offering himself to his Father in the Temple and offering himself to all mankind in the whole wide world.

Both offerings are done for him by his parents — he is still but a child. But what a contrast there is between these two offerings! It is a double mystery which St. Matthew and St. Luke, each from his own inspired point of view, give us to ponder in our hearts — as Mary and Joseph once pondered them.

The first mystery was all light: the rapturous reception in the Temple. And then, even while there, a shadow comes: Simeon's prophecy of a sword.

And then, sometime after the return to Bethlehem, the prophecy is fulfilled. It comes in the middle of the night: Joseph is awakened in his sleep by an angel. He must escape to Egypt immediately, for the Child's life is in danger.

Is Joseph's awakening only a dream? Outside the little house it is pitch dark and bitter cold, and Egypt is far away across a forbidding stretch of desert. No, he must go; he has no time to lose. He awakens Our Lady; she bundles up their little Child and some last-minute provisions, and the Holy Family departs into the unknown.

THE EXILE IN EGYPT

*[The angel said to Joseph]: "Remain [in Egypt]
until I tell you." . . . and [Joseph] remained there
until the death of Herod. (Mt 2:13, 15)*

SOUTH and west from the land of Judea lies the
Negeb, the broad base of the Holy Land. Farther
south is the desert of Sinai, and farther west is the
"Great Sea" curving toward Egypt. Across this frontier
of Asia facing the land bridge to Africa journeyed the
Holy Family on their way to exile.

They were retracing the path of the Patriarchs — the
seed of Abraham, the sons of Jacob — into that Egypt
where God had prepared, through the first Joseph, their
rescue from famine. It was a well-travelled highway,
this immemorial crossroads of the East; yet, as he
strode beside the little donkey carrying his wife and her
Child, the second Joseph must have seemed to himself
the merest speck of humanity, alone in a land no longer
holy, guided by neither star nor angel, into an exile of
empty waiting.

Where St. Joseph ended his journey, and where he
finally managed to get a house and set up a shop to shelter and support his little family, we do not know. It was
simply "Egypt," that name which fills the annals of the
Jews with such a mixture of fascination and dread.

Did the little Jesus splash his feet in the Nile, or gaze
upon the Pyramids? What impressed his imagination
through those years of his childhood? And indeed, how
many were those years? Again, we do not know. Nor
need we know, as long as we are certain that all is on
file in the archives of his Mother's heart.

THE HOLY INNOCENTS

*...Herod... was in a furious rage, and
he sent and killed all the male children in
Bethlehem and in all that region who were
two years old or under... (Mt 2:16)*

WHEN the Holy Family had finished their hurried
flight into Egypt and finally found somewhere to
stay in that strange teeming land, they must have had
some intimation of what lay behind them in Bethlehem. Given the monstrous reputation of King Herod
for fury and violence, St. Joseph and Our Lady could
only imagine how his soldiers were even then breaking
into houses and slaughtering in cold blood every baby
boy they found.

Yes, this was the price of their Child's rescue: so that
he could live, some dozens of little children were killed.

Yes, this was the "sword" foreseen by Simeon — and
what a "sign of contradiction" it really is! God's own
Son, powerless before a petty tyrant! And for this defeat
he pays with the blood of innocent babies and the tears
of their parents.

Being too young to exercise mind and will, the Holy
Innocents could not consciously and deliberately "witness" to Christ; they simply died in his place. What a
beginning for the salvation of the world!

But we are blessed if we are not scandalized by this
(cf. Mt 11:6). Long before St. Paul wrote about it, Our
Lady and St. Joseph in their Egyptian exile knew that
"the weakness of God is stronger than man" (1 Cor 1:25).
As they watched their little Son playing with his scruffy
peers in the refugee camp, they knew by faith what he
knew by vision: that those little boys back in Bethlehem
who died for him would live forever in heaven, because
he would someday die for them.

THE RETURN TO NAZARETH

*... an angel of the Lord appeared in a dream
to Joseph in Egypt, saying, "Rise, take the Child
and his mother, go to the land of Israel, for those
who sought the Child's life are dead." And he rose
and took the Child and his mother, and went to
the land of Israel... And he went and dwelt in
a city called Nazareth... (Mt 2:19–21, 23)*

THE infamous Herod who had ordered the murder
of his little rival, the newborn King of the Jews,
and had instead murdered the Holy Innocents, was now
himself dead. One of his sons succeeded to the throne,
a puppet kingship under the imperial power of Rome.

St. Joseph, once more at the word of an angel, set out
on a journey with the Child and his Mother, with their
little donkey and their meager possessions. This time it
was with relief and daylight that they went. However
long had been their exile, it was not soon enough to be
ended and to be back in their homeland, never again
to leave it.

St. Matthew sees in this journey of the Holy Family
the fulfillment of two prophecies. One relates to their
point of departure: "Out of Egypt I have called my
son" (Mt 2:15; Hos 11:1). Our Lord was to have personal
experience of the Exodus, that greatest single event of
the Old Testament: he was to relive his People's passage
from bondage into freedom in the Promised Land.

The other prophecy relates to their destination: not
back to Judea where he was born, but farther back to
Nazareth where he was conceived. "He shall be called
a Nazarene" (Mt 2:23). Thus would Jesus be identified
through all his earthly life, even to the Cross.

Indeed, the world's salvation could be nowhere better
prepared than in little Nazareth. For, hidden though it
was, it flanked the great caravan route from the North,
in a land that Isaiah called "Galilee of the Gentiles"
(Mt 4:15; Is 8:23).

THE MYSTERY OF
THE PRESENTATION

Hail Mary, full of grace, the Lord is with
thee, blessed art thou among women, and
blessed is the fruit of thy womb, Jesus.

THE Fourth Joyful Mystery of the Rosary is perhaps, of all the mysteries having to do with Our Lord's and his Mother's earthly lives, the most "composite." Blending the data of two disparate sources, St. Luke's and St. Matthew's Gospels, this Mystery relates Our Lord's Nativity with all that would follow in that one short life.

In both breadth and depth, the Mystery of the new-born Christ grows before our eyes. We see the stage expanded to lands unholy: the vast world of the Gentiles waiting for salvation. And even more, we see what that salvation will cost. The joys of Christmas and Epiphany come at a price: sorrow for the Savior and for all who share his life, beginning with his Mother.

Of her seven Sorrows, two are already here — in the very midst of her Joys! She is still a very young mother, still very likely in her teens. How many silent tears must she have already shed as she pondered this Mystery in her heart? Tears of joy and exultation, mingled with tears of fear and apprehension, marked the flow of these first precious years of her Child's life.

Their intermittent sunshine and shadow only heighten and deepen the constancy and faithfulness of the Handmaid of the Lord.

Holy Mary, Mother of God,
pray for us sinners, now and
at the hour of our death.
Amen.

THE FIFTH
JOYFUL MYSTERY

✠

THE FINDING OF OUR
LORD IN THE TEMPLE

THE FEAST OF THE PASSOVER

*... His parents went to Jerusalem every year at the
feast of the Passover. And when he was twelve years
old, they went up according to custom.* (Lk 2:41–42)

S T. Matthew closes his short narrative of Jesus's early
life with his return to Nazareth after the exile in
Egypt. St. Luke also emphasizes Nazareth as claiming
by far the greatest portion of Our Lord's earthly life.

But just as St. Luke began his Infancy Gospel in Jerusalem with the annunciation of St. John the Baptist, so
he concludes it with an incident that occurred also in
Jerusalem — the only recorded incident in a Hidden Life
that extended some twenty-five years or more. This
incident is the Fifth Joyful Mystery of the Rosary: the
Finding of Our Lord, at the age of twelve, in the Temple.

Explicitly remembered by Our Lady (cf. Lk 2:51),
this incident is pivotal. It gives us not only Our Lord's
first recorded words; it gives us the intent, the mission
that he sees in his human existence.

If the Temple was the heart and hearth of Judaism,
the celebration of the Passover was the heart and hearth
of the Temple. Here was fulfilled its primary purpose:
the offering of sacrifice to renew the Covenant by which
the People would return to their God and God would
remain with his People — the Covenant that was first
formally struck by Israel's "Passover" from Egypt to
the Promised Land. To celebrate this annual Passover,
the Holy Family now comes to the Temple in Jerusalem.

This year Jesus is with his parents for the first time
as one assuming his own responsibility for this sacred
action, for he is now twelve years old, the year of his
"Bar Mitzvah," his "Confirmation."

THE LOSING OF JESUS
IN JERUSALEM

When the feast was ended, as they were returning,
the boy Jesus stayed behind in Jerusalem.
When they did not find him, they returned
to Jerusalem seeking him. (Lk 2:43–45)

THIS incident presents a mystery of Christ that is mysterious indeed. How could it be that this Child, who now by virtue of his "rite of passage" in this year's Passover, is at least in some sense an "adult"— how could it be that he would deliberately desert his unsuspecting parents? How could he do this, knowing what awful pain he would cause them?

It has been said that of all Our Lady's Sorrows, this third Sorrow was the greatest. For in all the others she suffered with Jesus; now she suffers in his absence— and feels that this first-time absence must be in some way her fault. See her now, as in near panic she and St. Joseph retrace their day's journey back to a Jerusalem packed with noisy jostling pilgrims. They search everywhere, they inquire at the police stations, they plead for any scrap of information. They may even have gone back to the Temple to plead with God.

And Jesus meanwhile? It may well have been for him a matter of "hide and seek." See him darting through the streets, hiding from his parents—and seeking? Seeking perhaps some sites of pilgrimage of his own: a garden at the foot of Mount Olivet, a small hill to the west outside the city gates. In any case, he is not lost; he is only hiding! A mystery, after all, is only a "hiding" that will through "seeking" become a "finding."

Jesus will arrange his being found—in three days' time.

THE FINDING OF JESUS
IN THE TEMPLE

After three days they found him in the Temple...
(Lk 2:46)

IT is now the third day since they lost their Son, and Our Lady and St. Joseph go once more to the Temple. Suddenly they hear a voice — his voice! It comes from one of the chambers surrounding the Portico of Solomon (cf. Jn 10:23).

They edge near, and there he is! Sitting in what looks like an impromptu seminar, in the give-and-take of a scholarly discussion! His voice is still that of a child, but his poise! So gracious and manly — already as St. Luke would describe him years later in Nazareth (cf. Lk 4:22).

Then their eyes meet: mother and Son, and father and Son. And in that one moment, all the woe of the three days' loss is gone.

For all that, however, there is something new that that loss has brought, some new facet that Mary and Joseph had never seen before is now before them. Jesus is still their little Child — and will always be such, especially for his Mother. Yet now there is an air of mystery about him, and all the more so for his very candor and simplicity — his being totally "himself."

Whether they embrace right then and there we do not know. What we do know is that, beyond all such embraces, the souls of all three are caught up in a truly new communion of joy, than which nothing on this earth could be more total.

Yes, the rapture of this face-to-face finding of Jesus by Mary and Joseph is but the reflection of his rapture at revealing this new "finding" to them.

JESUS AMONG THE TEACHERS

... they found him ... sitting among the teachers,
listening to them and asking them questions;
and all who heard him were amazed at his
understanding and his answers. (Lk 2:46–47)

IN his brief account of this one event in Our Lord's
Hidden Life, which the Holy Spirit and Our Lady
disclosed to him, St. Luke pauses to mention a detail
that he must have considered significant enough to
be included. He carefully notes not only Our Lord's
presence among the *didaskoloi* — the "teachers" — in the
Temple, but also his interaction with them.

Both he and they are listening and speaking in turn,
and his speech — like theirs — is both questioning and
answering. What a dialogue this must have been! A
twelve-year-old boy, not standing (as is proper to a
pupil), but sitting (as teachers sit, cf. Mt 5:1), *en meso* —
in the center of the "faculty" of the central institution
of all Judaism, the Temple itself!

Let it not be said that the Rosary omits the public life
of our Lord Jesus Christ! For the public life is included
in the Luminous Mysteries given to us by St. John Paul
II in 2002 (see the Third Luminous Mystery: Jesus's
Proclamation of the Kingdom of God).

But here in miniature in St. Luke's Gospel is the
essential ministry of those few decisive years between
his Hidden Life and his Last Passover, in which he was,
first and last, a Teacher. his habitual title is "Rabbi" or
Didaskolos or *Magister* (in the three languages of his
Cross) or — as we used to say in English — "Master."

Our Lord here begins his formal teaching ministry
and thus anticipates what would be his own summary
of his career in this world: "I was with you daily teaching in the Temple" (Mt 26:55; cf. Lk 19:47; Jn 18:20).
Yes, this self-revelation of Jesus as Teacher must ever
remain *en meso* of our hearts, if we are to see Jesus as
his Mother saw him on that unforgettable day.

JESUS AND MARY IN DIALOGUE

... His mother said to him, "Son, why have you treated
us so? Behold, your father and I have been seeking
You in sorrow." And he said to them, "How is it that
you sought me? Did you not know that I must be in
my Father's house?" And they did not understand
the saying which he spoke to them. (Lk 2:48–50)

THE thrilling sensation at finding her Son — and
in these surroundings — quietly subsided, and
now Mary speaks. What words can she find for such
a moment? The antecedent sorrow is still there, for it
too was caught up in the wonder that engulfed them.

And so she asks her Son a question, a question wrung
from her heart, with a candor and simplicity matching
his. It is a simple "why?" She speaks for St. Joseph —
"your father" — as well as for herself. Indeed, she speaks
for all mankind, from the heart of our common nature,
bonded as it is by family ties.

So natural in fact is this question "why?" that Jesus
himself will ask of God essentially the same question as
he is dying: "Why have You abandoned me?" (Mt 27:46;
Mk 15:34).

What are the feelings of the Heart of Jesus at these
words of his Mother? He must have recognized in her
all the mingled joys and sorrows of the whole human
family, filtered and enlivened in her purest of hearts.

Yet he also knows, by his vision of his Father which
she cannot share, that she has yet to reach that fullest
human understanding of his Mystery which he has
destined exclusively for her. Until then he must remain
silent — alone with his Father.

So too must remain the mystery — the "hiding and
seeking," the "losing and finding" — which is indeed
the quintessential paradox of the Gospel (cf. Mt 10:39;
16:25; Mk 8:35; Lk 9:24; Jn 12:25). But in one respect,
Jesus already shares a full certainty with Mary — and
she with him: their hearts are indissolubly one.

THE HIDDEN LIFE
OF OUR LORD

... and he went down with them and came to
Nazareth, and was obedient to them. (Lk 2:51)

FOLLOWING that one-sentence answer to his
Mother's question, the Boy Jesus is silent, and, for
the official record of his Gospel, will remain so for the
next eighteen years. St. Luke tells us simply that with
his parents he left the Temple (were the rabbis still
assembled and watching, and wondering in their turn?)
and once more took the road back north to Galilee.

So begins by far the longest period of Our Lord's
earthly life. What did their fellow Nazarenes know
or think of the Holy Family? As in most small towns
everywhere, it must have evened out to something like
the universal average: everyone in town knew everything — and nothing — about them (cf. Mt 13:53–58;
Mk 6:1–6; Lk 4:16–30; Jn 7:3–9).

The only thing in this silence that St. Luke notes
is Our Lord's obedience. His life is simply the Fourth
Commandment lived perfectly. His immediate service to
his Father in the Temple is now mediated in his service
to Our Lady and St. Joseph at home.

The "higher" vocation, such as his cousin John was
pursuing in the desert (cf. Lk 1:80), yielded to the
"lower" vocation, such as the vast majority of mankind
was pursuing, then and now.* This is his vocation too:
to live the life of a common laborer, neither wealthy
nor indigent, with its even cadence of work and rest,
conversation and silence, recreation and prayer.

Such is the life of him who chose only what his
Father chose for him for that time: that he be "the
carpenter's son" (Mt 13:55).

---

* See Puhl, *The Spiritual Exercises of St. Ignatius*, no. 135.

THE GROWTH OF OUR LORD

And Jesus increased in wisdom and in stature,
and in favor with God and man. (Lk 2:52)

THE Holy House of Nazareth was indeed an invio-
lable sanctuary for just the three of them; it had to
be, even naturally, for every husband and father should
have his castle. Yet all four Gospels tell us that there
were relatives around; and so there was an intermediate level between the "cloister" of the Three alone and
the come-and-go of Joseph's customers and Mary's
companions at the well. There were also the cousins
(cf. Mt 13:55; Mk 6:3).

Nothing better records the passage of time than the
measurements of children as they grow. And Jesus grew.
This year he is taller than his cousin James; next year
he will be taller than his mother!

So Jesus grew—through the teens and in the twen-
ties—tall and straight like his father, and in looks and
sensibilities how like his mother!

Matching his physical age is his "wisdom": his
knowledge of nature, the weather and the landscape,
the plants and animals, the "human condition" of the
"global village."

And matching both his wisdom and age is his "grace."
Ah, once more we touch the core of the Mystery of
Christ. Now he is the "altar boy" in the synagogue,
reciting his Psalms of Hallel. Now he is at home with
his parents, musing on a passage of the Scriptures. Now
he is all alone on a hilltop, alone with his Father in
heaven.

In his human heart the Eternal Word of the Father
grows: ever immeasurably deeper in the Love that is
the single Spirit of Father and Son.

THE DEATH OF ST. JOSEPH

*Jesus, when he began his ministry, was
about thirty years of age, being the son [as
was supposed] of Joseph . . . (Lk 3:23)*

AFTER Jesus and Mary, the person most present in
the five Joyful Mysteries of the Rosary is St. Joseph.
This is, of course, as it should be. From his espousal
with Our Lady before the Annunciation to his return
to Nazareth after the Finding in the Temple, St. Joseph
is there — by responsibility and by right — at the side of
Our Lady and her Son.

Yet for all that, his presence is rarely prominent, and
his voice is never heard. Watchful and silent, resourceful
and reserved, Joseph is indeed the "just man" *par excellence* of the Scriptural tradition: the perfect custodian
of God's dearest treasures, utterly faithful to the last.

That St. Joseph did not survive Our Lord's Hidden
Life is certain, although there is no explicit mention
in the Gospels of this fact. Implicitly, Our Lady is portrayed by all the Evangelists as a widow. This makes
Our Lord's eventual departure from Nazareth all the
more poignant for her.

But as for St. Joseph's departure, its fittingness is
clear. After all, his one life's mission had been accomplished: he had brought up his son Jesus to man's full
estate. St. Joseph never witnessed a miracle nor heard a
discourse from Jesus; seemingly, he died as he had lived,
on the threshold of the New Testament.

But it was truly within this New and Eternal Testament that he had his happy death. For, though he was
carried to the bosom of Abraham (cf. Lk 16:22), the last
persons he beheld on earth in his dying embrace were
Jesus and Mary.

THE BAPTISM OF OUR LORD

*In those days Jesus came from Nazareth of Galilee and
was baptized by John in the Jordan. And when he came
up out of the water, immediately he saw the heavens
opened and the Spirit descending upon him like a dove;
and a voice came from heaven, "Thou art my beloved
Son, with Thee I am well pleased." (Mk 1:9–10)*

SO begins the definitive ministry for which Jesus had
come to earth, foreshadowed eighteen years earlier,
now made real. Not totally real, for there remains another
baptism wherewith he is to be baptized: his baptism of
blood — which is the New Testament (cf. Lk 12:50).

Yet this baptism of water to which he now goes is the
formal inauguration of his mission as "the Christ." It
takes place near Jericho in Judea, beside the river Jordan,
where his cousin John, prophetically preaching repen-
tance, now awaits him.

All three Synoptics relate the three essential details
of what happens: Our Lord's going into and coming
out of the water, the Holy Spirit's descending upon
him as a dove from an opened heaven, and the Father's
addressing Jesus as his beloved Son.

This momentous event is the first formal revelation of
the Blessed Trinity. It is revealed not so much in its eternity as in its action in time: the Father as anointing, the
Son as the Anointed One, the Holy Spirit as the Ointment.

This overture to Our Lord's ministry as "the Christ"
completes his thirty years of hidden preparation; it is
the mystery of the Epiphany — the "Manifestation" —
achieved.

Now there is but one detail missing: Our Lady is not
here.* We may say, of course, that she did not need it;
she had her own revelation of the Trinity at the Annunciation. We may also say that Our Lord was holding in
reserve for her the culmination of his Epiphany, which
would come anon!

---

* See Puhl, *The Spiritual Exercises of St. Ignatius*, no. 273.

THE WEDDING FEAST AT CANA

*... there was a marriage at Cana in Galilee, and the
mother of Jesus was there; Jesus was also invited to
the marriage, with his disciples.... The mother of
Jesus said to him, "They have no wine."
... His mother said to the servants, "Do whatever
he tells you." This, the first of his signs, Jesus
did at Cana in Galilee, and manifested his glory;
and his disciples believed in him.*
(Jn 2:1–3, 5, 11)

THE three Synoptics round out the mystery of Our
Lord's baptism by telling us of his forty days' fast
in the Judean desert, where his Sonship (and implicitly
his title of "the Christ") were tested by Satan.

St. John, the fourth Evangelist, rounds out the same
mystery by telling us what happened when he returned
to Galilee from the desert to begin his ministry of pro-
claiming his Father's Kingdom. For this occasion he
chose a wedding feast not far from his hometown and
with his Mother present. From a fast and a miracle
refused (cf. Mt 4:3–4; Lk 4:3–4) to a feast and a miracle performed (cf. Jn 2:7–9), Jesus completes his manifestation—his Epiphany—and thus completes the Joyful
Mysteries of his Mother's Rosary.

Weddings are meant to be joyful occasions, and this
one is doubly so because of a potential embarrassment
averted ("they have no wine") and an unexpected
bounty provided ("you have saved the best wine until
now")—both through the thoughtful intercession of
Our Lady. She proves herself a true mother to the young
newlyweds—a happy augury of her universal motherhood to come.

But she did so as his Mother, as one who already
"believed in him": his interests, his "hour," his "glory."
He alone would determine when that "hour" would
come, when that "glory" would appear—she left that
wholly in his hands ("do whatever he tells you").

So his Epiphany in the water of the Jordan is now enhanced by his Epiphany in the wine of Cana — and this is done by virtue of her presence: the ever-faithful Handmaid of the Lord, and "Cause of all our joy"!

THE MYSTERY OF THE
FINDING OF OUR LORD

*Hail Mary, full of grace, the Lord is with
thee, blessed art thou among women, and
blessed is the fruit of thy womb, Jesus.*

WITH our fiftieth Hail Mary we have completed
the first "crown" of the whole Rosary that is the
Joyful Mysteries. We now add an extra Hail Mary to
summarize the fifth decade, which in turn summarizes
all five decades of this "crown."

It is a grand "recapitulation," bringing us right back
to where we began. We began with God foreseeing Mary
from eternity as the Mother of his Son. From her being
foreseen came her creation in grace as the "Immaculata." And from that creation came her "re-creation":
her "seed" and the crushing of the serpent's head (cf.
Gen 3:15; Rom 8:29–30).

After all the comings and goings, the words and the
silences, the lights and the shadows, the "hidings" and
the "findings" of these thirty years of the Word made
Flesh, we come back once more to Jesus and his Mother
in the crowning mystery of the wedding feast. Here we
have her last recorded words in Sacred Scripture: "Do
whatever he tells you" (Jn 2:5).

These words echo the words of the ancient wisdom
ascribed to her by the Church's liturgy: "And now,
my son, listen to me; happy are those who keep my
ways ... for he who finds me finds life, and obtains
favors from the Lord" (Prov 8:32).

*Holy Mary, Mother of God,
pray for us sinners, now and
at the hour of our death.
Amen.*

THE
SORROWFUL
MYSTERIES

THE FIRST
SORROWFUL MYSTERY

✠

THE AGONY
OF OUR LORD
IN THE GARDEN

THE LAST SUPPER

Now before the feast of the Passover, when Jesus
knew that his hour had come to depart out of this
world to the Father, having loved his own who were
in the world, he loved them to the end. (Jn 13:1)

THE Joyful Mysteries of the Rosary ended with a
banquet, which the Church's sacred liturgy has
always regarded as the culmination of the Epiphany,
when Our Lord, at the request of his Mother, performed his first miracle, began his public ministry, and
so manifested his glory (cf. Jn 2:11).

Some three years followed, years of teaching and
healing in a medley of joy and sorrow. Now at last, on
the eve of the Passover in Jerusalem, the "hour" anticipated at Cana has finally come. Now begin the Sorrowful Mysteries of the Rosary, and they begin with a
banquet: the Last Supper of Jesus and the Twelve.

In a spacious upper room we see them now. It is evening, and quiet has descended on the Holy City. This
solemn quiet of Passover pervades the room as Jesus
begins the supper.

"With desire have I desired to eat this Pasch with you
before I suffer" (Lk 22:15). What is this "desire" that
he identifies with this supper? Here at this very table,
the Apostles themselves do not really understand; Jesus
tells them so. Only later would they understand — after
he would leave them on the morrow (cf. Jn 15:25–26).

But now he cannot wait; he must give himself to
them before he gives himself to his enemies and to death.
"Take and eat; this is my Body broken for you . . . take
and drink; this is my Blood poured out for you."

And then he says: "Do this in memory of me"
(Lk 22:19–20).*

---

* See also Puhl, *The Spiritual Exercises of St. Ignatius*, no. 289.

GETHSEMANE

When they had sung a hymn, they went
out to the Mount of Olives . . . to a place
called Gethsemane . . . (Mt 26:30, 36)

AFTER his institution of the Holy Eucharist and
his farewell discourse to his Apostles, Our Lord
leaves the supper room to begin his Passion. He crosses
the silent city, past the Temple glistening cold in the
moonlight, and into the dark valley of Kedron. There,
at the foot of Mount Olivet, he enters a garden, a little
walled orchard of olive trees. The light of the full Paschal moon makes the tree shadows all the darker.

Their hushed walk stops as Jesus turns to the Eleven
and quietly speaks to them: "Sit here while I go yonder
to pray" (Mt 26:30).

This garden of Gethsemane, this olive grove beneath
the city wall, evokes the entire story of our redemption.
That story began in a garden, the Eden of our first parents; and it will end also in a garden lying outside the
wall on the other side of the city: the garden of the
Resurrection.

Right here in Gethsemane, Jesus speaks of that ending: "After I am risen, I will go before you into Galilee"
(Mt 26:32).

But in the meantime he must suffer — suffer as no
man had ever suffered or would ever suffer after. All
suffering will be his before the next day is done. And it
will begin — if it had not already begun — this very night.

So, "even unto death" (Mt 26:38), the Man of Sorrows walks into the depths of Gethsemane.

THE PRAYER OF JESUS

[Jesus] began to be greatly distressed and troubled.
And he said to [his disciples]: "my soul is very
sorrowful even to death; remain here and
watch." And going a little farther, he fell on
the ground and prayed... (Mk 14:33–35)

NOW in the depths of the garden, Jesus turns to the three disciples he took with him. His face and whole demeanor suddenly change. His habitual composure has vanished. He trembles. He looks anxiously, now at them, now away from them into the shadows, now back to them.

"Stay here and watch," he pleads, then withdrawing a short distance he falls to the ground, flat on his face. Peter, James, and John look on in stupefaction. Some months before, they had seen him transfigured in glory. Now they see a Transfiguration in reverse. Appalled, they hear him groaning — or is it now a cry?

"My Father, remove this chalice from me!" he moans, his voice muffled in the earth. Then, into the eerie moonlight above his head: "Yet if I must drink it, Thy will be done!" (Mt 26:39).

What a prayer is this! How utterly fearful, weak, and broken it is ... He repeats his plea — and his resignation — as if to fix them firmly. But they seem to slip, as once more to the ground he slumps.

"You will be scandalized in me this night" (Mt 26:31) he had warned his disciples after the supper. And here it is: the scandal, the shame, the humiliation.

How long does this last, this utterly unutterable prayer of Christ? The three disciple-witnesses cannot tell us, for in their stupor they have fallen asleep. All alone now, Jesus prays on.

THE ANGEL OF THE AGONY

*And there appeared to him an angel from
heaven, strengthening him. (Lk 22:43)*

OUR Lord had sought some human companionship in Gethsemane, but it had failed him; the three chosen disciples are asleep. However, another companionship is his: an angel has come from heaven, not to remove the chalice but to strengthen him for a contest of wills concerning that chalice.

For the angel sees another person there. Confronting Jesus in the darkest depth of the garden is another angel: the Enemy. As St. Luke had noted earlier, when Satan first tempted Jesus in the desert, "the devil departed from him until an opportune time" (Lk 4:13). Now is that time, when Jesus at his weakest meets Satan at his strongest, to settle once and for all whose world this shall be.

The Passion of Our Lord has, from its outset, a cosmic dimension. If we ourselves, as St. Paul warns us, "are not contending against flesh and blood, but against the principalities, against the powers, against the world rulers of this present darkness, against the spiritual hosts of wickedness in the heavenly places" (Eph 6:12), how much unimaginably more must have been his battle that night!

There was no massing of the legions — angels, good and bad, in their myriads — that night in Gethsemane. Only one good angel is there — as a kind of "second" — to witness the Man Jesus and the Angel Lucifer in single combat. At its outcome on the morrow, a universe will be redeemed.

THE AGONY OF JESUS

And being in agony, he prayed more earnestly;
and his sweat became like great drops of blood
falling down upon the ground. (Lk 22:44)

THE actual combat is now described by St. Luke in one clause. *Prolixius orabat* — "He prayed more earnestly" — or, in an older version, "He prayed the longer." The undulations of his body, now writhing, now prostrate, now "in loud cries and tears" (Heb 5:7), now in soft plaintive sighs, seem now to cease. His body responds in fixity to his spirit: like a statue in the shadows, he kneels before his invisible Father in total silence.

Then, slowly but steadily, there appear on his garments spreading splotches of red: he is sweating blood. Yes, his first bleeding in his Passion is spontaneous and from within. Before anyone has laid a hand on him, he cannot wait to begin the pouring out of the price of our redemption.

Here, literally, is the wine press of the prophecy (cf. Is 63:2–3). But it is not the wrath of God pressing on Jesus that causes this blood to flow. Rather, it is the love of God that crushes him.

He is the Beloved Son in whom the Father is well pleased (cf. Mk 1:11), the One who always does only what his Father does (cf. Jn 5:19), whose very words are not his but his Father's (cf. Jn 17:8). His love for men which brought him down from heaven was his Father's love for men that gave him to the world (cf. Jn 3:16).

No, it is not some monstrous wrath of a vengeful God exacting payment from the all-innocent One. It is rather his Father's love that overwhelms him now. God's love, spurned and unrequited by men, brims all the more in the Heart of Christ. And it spills forth — bright red in the depths of Gethsemane.

THE SLEEPING DISCIPLES

And he came and found them sleeping, and he said to Peter, "Simon, are you asleep? Could you not stay awake one hour [with me]?" (Mk 14:37)

WHILE St. Luke notes the presence of an angel at Our Lord's agony, St. Matthew and St. Mark note the presence of his chosen companions: Peter, James, and John. Or rather, it is their absence that is noted.

Three times, we are told, had Jesus come back to them from his prayer, only to find them sleeping. What a sight it must have been to them when at last he awoke them. Their sleep-drugged vision grasps no angel—good or bad—nor even any man. Stark in the moonlight, what they see is "a worm and no man" (Ps 21/22:6). His face hidden, his garments stained, "only Jesus" (Mk 9:8) stands before them: the literal fulfillment of the prophesied "Suffering Servant of Yahweh."

Out of the shadows of that shaming moment we hear him now, speaking to us as he once spoke to them: "Could you not watch one hour with me?" In his mind that night, Jesus no doubt saw the many nights thereafter when his sacramental presence in our churches would be bereft of human company.

And so his preparation for his sacrifice on the morrow would be unattended. Could this inattention lead to his being totally ignored? Lest it be so, he asks us now to make, at least from time to time, a "holy hour" with him—in his Holy Eucharist, in his Heart.*

---

* See Puhl, *The Spiritual Exercises of St. Ignatius*, no. 195.

JUDAS'S BETRAYAL

*. . . there came a crowd, and the man called Judas
was leading them. He drew near to Jesus to kiss
him; but Jesus said to him, "Judas, would you betray
the Son of man with a kiss?" (Lk 22:47–48)*

THERE were three Apostles chosen by Our Lord to be his companions in the farther reaches of the garden, and there were eight other Apostles left by him at the entrance to the garden to "watch and pray." There was one more Apostle not accounted for. Judas was last seen leaving the supper room before Our Lord had spoken his farewell discourse.

Had he left before Jesus had instituted the Holy Eucharist — and the Priesthood? Whether as a priest or not, Judas was "one of the Twelve." And as such — as a most privileged intimate and friend — Judas went out into the night (cf. Jn 13:30) to betray his Master.

We see him now, alert and watchful, leading a band of "security agents" from the Sanhedrin to apprehend Jesus in his accustomed place of prayer (cf. Lk 22:39). The torchlight and footsteps arouse the Apostles and they gather around Jesus, who has come out of the recesses of the garden to meet the men accompanying Judas.

The traitor approaches Jesus and greets him with a kiss. Jesus speaks quietly to Judas; he calls him by his name as a friend (cf. Mt 26:50). Is this what he has come for, to betray him? Judas shrinks back into the band, away from his brother Apostles and from Jesus — never to see them again.

And so the deed is done. Jesus faces his enemies, betrayed by his friend.

THE APOSTLES' DESERTION

. . . they all forsook him and fled.
(Mk 14:50)

JUDAS'S treason may have been worth it to Jesus's enemies; at least he found Jesus for them. But Our Lord was not handed over by Judas. He himself did the handing over. As St. John recounted, he faced down the whole crowd of them; in fact, at the initial shock of his presence they all fell down.

He waits for them to regain their feet, and then he gives them the terms of his surrender: "If you seek me, let these men go" (Jn 18:8). Thus he fulfills two things he had spoken of earlier: he will give himself up of his own accord (cf. Jn 10:8), and he will not lose anyone whom his Father had given him (cf. Jn 17:12).

Our Lord's mastery of this moment cannot disguise, however, its poignancy. His majestic calm contrasts with the unseemly scuffle that ensues: an aroused Simon Peter lays about him with a sword — and severs an enemy ear. Jesus reprimands him and repairs the damage; it is his last miracle of healing (cf. Lk 22:51).

Then, we are told, "all the disciples forsook him and fled" (Mt 26:56). What is Our Lord's thought — and feeling — at this event? Is it a departure by his permission? Or a desertion to his grief? It is both, as earlier that very night he had said to them, "The hour is coming, it has indeed now come, when you will be scattered, every man to his own, and you will leave me alone; yet I am not alone, for the Father is with me" (Jn 16:32).

THE HOUR OF DARKNESS

... this is your hour, and the power of darkness.
(Lk 22:53)

OUR Lord had said to his Apostles when they first entered Gethsemane some hours — a seeming eternity — before, "My soul is sorrowful even unto death" (Mt 26:38; Mk 14:34). Now, alone and surrounded by enemies, the Man of Sorrows gives voice to what he faces.

Gone are the days of his action-filled ministry — his journeyings and his healings, his preachings — especially there in the Temple, high across the valley silhouetted against the moon. And even his prayings, here in this very garden, now steeped in the shadows of his soul.

Of all these things, so vital in their time, he is now bereft. Erect and motionless, with the calm of utter fatigue, he surrenders himself to his captors.

Jesus effects his surrender by a simple statement. They had come out after him "as against a thief, with swords and clubs" (Mt 26:55; Mk 14:48). This indignity was uncalled for; he gives himself up freely, willing what his Father has willed, "that the Scriptures might be fulfilled" (Mt 26:56; Mk 14:49).

Yes, the Servant of Yahweh is now ready: his "hour" has brought him to this moment. Now, by his leave, their "hour" can begin. He calls this hour of theirs "the power of darkness." A "power" seemingly irresistible and supreme — and a "darkness" straight from hell.

Their action will be his Passion, for he will now simply "take it" until he dies.

THE MYSTERY OF THE
AGONY IN THE GARDEN

*Hail Mary, full of grace, the Lord is with
thee, blessed art thou among women, and
blessed is the fruit of thy womb, Jesus.*

THIS Mystery of Our Lord's Prayer and Agony in
the Garden is more than just a great overture to
the Passion. It is, in a sense, the entire Passion. (Indeed,
counting in its first Hail Mary, it contains the entire Passion, beginning to end — sacramentally.) For already his
soul is sealed "even until death." There remains but the
execution of his Body and the total effusion of his Blood.

But there is another aspect of this Mystery that
makes it almost unique in the entirety of the Rosary
itself. Here, for the first time, Our Lady is not present.
Although she was surely in Jerusalem that night, she
was neither at the Last Supper nor in Gethsemane.

Our Lord had evidently willed it that way, and whatever he said to do she did (cf. Jn 2:5). What a consolation
her presence, in both places or in either of them, would
have been to him!

But no, this would be part of his "chalice" that for
now must be his alone. She would be with him on the
morrow; but for now he must be hidden from her —
and she from him — in order that the sorrows of both,
even before their ending, would be complete.

*Holy Mary, Mother of God,
pray for us sinners, now and
at the hour of our death.
Amen.*

THE SECOND
SORROWFUL MYSTERY

✠

THE SCOURGING
OF OUR LORD
AT THE PILLAR

THE ARREST OF JESUS

*... the band of soldiers and their captain and the
officers of the Jews seized Jesus and bound him.
First they led him to Annas... (Jn 18:12 – 13)*

THE "hour" in which Our Lord put himself into
the hands of sinners (cf. Mk 14:41) must have been
around midnight. Until then he had, of course, been
with sinners — indeed, the only sinless one, his Mother,
was singularly absent.

But the only sinner who, as a sinner, actually touched
him as yet was Judas. Now, however, he would be with
sinners — evil men — as immediately and intently as he
was with the evil spirits in Gethsemane.

Now under arrest, his hands bound behind his back,
Jesus is hurried along by the Temple guard, back to the
fateful city where the mass of the citizenry and pilgrims
are asleep — while a select few are not.

The first stop is at the house of Annas, the father-in-
law of the High Priest and the recognized, albeit unofficial, leader of the "establishment." He interrogates the
Prisoner about his "establishment": the "doctrine" and
the "disciples" that this young unconventional rabbi
has formed.

At Jesus's reply that this teaching of his was no con-
spiracy but was open to all, one of the guards struck him
in the face (Jn 18:22). Here is the first clear-cut injury to
his body coming from without. See him stagger back-
wards from this sudden attack, handcuffed as he is, and
now with blood on his face and in his eyes.

Its mark of stinging pain and disfigurement will
remain there throughout his Passion — just as it remains
there to this day, imprinted on his shroud.

JESUS BEFORE THE SANHEDRIN

*... they led Jesus to the high priest; and
all the chief priests and the elders and the
scribes were assembled. (Mk 14:53)*

F ROM the house of Annas, the manacled Prisoner
is hustled off to the nearby house of Caiaphas, the
titular High Priest, where the Sanhedrin, the highest
governing body of the Jews, had been hastily assembled. It is an emergency session that cannot wait for
the morrow; it would be unseemly to conduct such a
trial as they had in mind at this very time of Passover.

For this is a deadly business tonight: a young upstart
rabbi from Galilee has come to the capital city to challenge the "establishment" head-on by his claim to be
the "Hosanna-ed" Messiah himself. They will charge
him with blasphemy, the most heinous of capital crimes.
They will secure his admission to the charge under
oath—and so this "Son of God" will be handed over
to the Romans for the execution of the death penalty.

Although unnerved by the Prisoner's serene and
silent waiver of his defenses, Caiaphas yet manages to
wrest his verdict without a hitch (cf. Mk 14:61–62).
Jesus stands self-condemned: he is indeed the Son of
the Living God.

Only later will the members of this court—along
with all mankind—see this truth for themselves. See
him now in this literally most critical moment of his
earthly life. Hands bound behind his back, he stands in
the center of the courtroom, in the glow of oil lamps.

Taunted by the High Priest and his confreres, Jesus
once more has his face disfigured. First it was by a
lackey's fist; now it is by priestly mouths—as one after
another the judge and jury spit on him (cf. Mk 14:65).

PETER'S DENIAL

Peter followed him at a distance, right into the
courtyard of the high priest.... And he began to
invoke a curse on himself and to swear, "I do not
know this man of whom you speak." (Mk 14:54, 71)

WHILE the trial of Our Lord is taking place in the house of Caiaphas, another drama is underway in an outer courtyard of that house. Simon Peter has managed to get into the courtyard "to see the end" (Mt 26:58). The night is cold, and a fire is blazing in the courtyard — and there stands Peter in the firelight.

He is recognized as being one of Jesus's disciples, and is so accosted by a servant girl. Peter is caught off guard. Spontaneous as he had always been in his faith and love for Jesus, Peter now abruptly disclaims any knowledge — much less love — for him. In fact, in his panic he repeats his denial, not once but twice, and by oath!

All four Evangelists recount this threefold denial of Our Lord by St. Peter. As much as the sin of Judas — indeed if not more than it — the sin of Peter is seared in the memory of the Church. It marks the ultimate hurt to Jesus — and the ultimate ruin to oneself.

Yet now, another spontaneity, surpassing all that has yet happened — for good or ill — that night, is spotted by St. Luke. Our Lord, crossing the courtyard from his trial to his prison cell for the remainder of the night, turns to Peter — and looks at him (Lk 22:61). It lasts but a second or two, but it is enough.

What must have passed between those two faces — those two hearts — in that split second! Leaving the scene immediately, Peter bursts into tears — the bittersweet tears of instant conversion.

JESUS BEFORE PILATE

. . . they led Jesus from the house of Caiaphas
to the Praetorium. . . . Pilate went out to
them and said, "What accusation do you
bring against this man?" (Jn 18:28–29)

IN the pre-dawn darkness of that first Good Friday,
two sounds were heard: the crowing of a rooster and
the sobbing of a broken man. Poor penitent Peter must
have wandered the night — and now?

At the first faint light in the East, the Holy City
bestirs itself to what will be the most momentous day
in all history. The day begins with a delegation from the
Sanhedrin calling on the de facto sovereign, to execute
the verdict of the previous night's session. Caesar's sov-
ereignty is represented and exercised by his procurator
of Judea, one Pontius Pilate.

Flanked by the eagles of his office, symbols of the
might and majesty of Rome, Pontius Pilate strides out
onto the balcony of the Praetorium, the towered quar-
ters of the imperial power designed to overawe the Temple area and the city below.

His haughty mien belies a faint sense of insecurity;
already he has run afoul of these strange people and
their strange religion. He must remain aloof and judi-
cious, letting the impersonal machinery of the Roman
law work out its justice.

Little does he know that the Man thrust forward
to be judged by him will reverse their respective roles.
Jesus, by submitting to Pilate's power, will be Pilate's
judge. And by that judgment, Pilate will be remembered
in history for this one event alone: that under him by
name — *sub Pontio Pilato* — the Passion of Jesus Christ
reached its term.

JESUS BEFORE HEROD

[Pilate] sent him over to Herod. . . . And Herod with
his soldiers treated him with contempt and mocked
him . . . and sent him back to Pilate. (Lk 23:7, 11)

AT a certain moment in this confrontation between the Roman governor and the Jewish officials, an opening appears whereby an awkward impasse can be avoided. The accusation against Jesus is no longer his claim to be the Son of God; rather, it is his claim to be the King of the Jews.

No matter that the two claims intersect; it is now more politic to stress the political over the religious. And happily for all concerned, an appropriate judge acceptable to both parties happens to be available. Herod Antipas, the degenerate son of Herod the Great and the puppet of the Romans for the administration of Galilee, is in town. Let this half-Jew have the compliment — and the responsibility — of judging Jesus. A sensible solution, this — if only the Prisoner, in his own best interest, will cooperate.

So now he stands, shackled and silent, before the man whose father had once sought to kill him for being the King of the Jews, and who himself had killed John the Baptist for being that King's herald.

But John's death had troubled Herod; it was really his wife's doing, for he himself was beset with fears — the murky fears of one sated with lusts and impervious to any word with even the least glimmer of spirit.

Given this horror of a dead soul before him, Jesus says nothing. He can only look on Herod with infinite pity. And for the pains of his pity he is mocked — and contemptuously sent back to Pilate.

JESUS AND BARABBAS

*. . . Pilate said to [the crowd]: "Whom do you
want me to release to you, Barabbas or Jesus
who is called the Christ?" (Mt 27:17)*

THE foolish futile detour across town to the house
of Herod has taken an hour or so; it is now near
the "third hour" — nine o'clock — and the word is out
that the wonder-worker prophet from Nazareth is on
trial for his life.

The Paschal crowds converge on the great square facing the governor's residence, while inside the governor
paces back and forth irresolutely. Jesus is once again
back on his hands, and tension builds between the two
silences — Jesus's and his own — as the muffled murmur
of the mob outside slowly mounts. This is the setting
for an event recounted by all four Evangelists (the first
such since Peter's denial) as leading to the climax of
Our Lord's trial before Pilate.

Whether the initiative for this event lay with the governor or with the crowd is not clear; but that in itself
is significant. For the real initiative may be ascribed to
the Prince of Darkness, who even after Gethsemane is
still probing Jesus's identity.

Suddenly a new option occurs to Pilate: he can grant
clemency at Paschal time to any one prisoner facing the
death penalty. Thus, he can release Jesus (and so satisfy
his near conviction that Jesus is innocent) by contrasting him with a particularly dangerous and despicable
prisoner named Barabbas.

Barabbas! The name means "son of the father." The
Jewish leaders see the point and incite a shout: "Barabbas is our true 'Christ'! Release our true 'Paschal victim'!
And as for this Jesus — this 'anti-Christ' — away with
him!"

PRELUDE TO THE SCOURGING

*[Pilate said to the chief priests and the rulers and
the people:] "Behold, I do not find this man guilty of
any of the charges against him. . . . I will therefore
chastise him and release him." (Lk 23:14, 16)*

WITH Herod's remanding of Jesus and the crowd's
demanding of Barabbas, Pilate sees himself facing
a dreadful dilemma: on the one hand, he is now fully
convinced that Jesus is innocent; on the other hand, he
is equally convinced that the mob is implacable — innocent or not, Jesus must die.

With surly desperation he retreats to compromise:
he will punish Jesus and then release him. The punishment will be subjecting the Prisoner to the *flagellum*: not
the strictly limited whipping allowed under Jewish law
(cf. 2 Cor 11:24), but rather the kind of beating under
Roman custom inflicted on any low-born alien already
marked for execution, and limited only by the victim's
not dying under the lash.

So Jesus is taken downstairs to a torture chamber, is
forced to disrobe, and is tied to a post. Thus the scene
is set for what is surely the most hideous suffering
endured by Our Lord — in soul and body — this side of
the Cross itself.

As the torturers limber up their lead-studded whips —
fiendish looking instruments of pain exceeding in inge-
nuity the cat-o'-nine tails of later times — what must be
Our Lord's thoughts and feelings as he waits for them
to begin? He stands stripped, at once stretched out and
bent against the cold stone pillar with its iron rings
gripping his wrists and ankles.

In his mind he cannot but reflect on the horren-
dous injustice of it: he is to suffer this precisely because
he is innocent! Meanwhile, in his sensibilities he feels
the awful shame of it — and, at any moment now, the
wracking pain.

THE SCOURGING OF JESUS

Pilate took Jesus and scourged him. (Jn 19:1)

THE scourging begins. Not one of the Evangelists describes it. In fact, the three Synoptics treat it rather obliquely. St. Matthew and St. Mark mention it only as a kind of preliminary to crucifixion (Mt 27:26; Mk 15:15), while St. Luke seems almost to suggest that it didn't happen at all, it having been Pilate's last vain attempt at compromise (Lk 23:22).

Yet all three list it as explicitly foreseen by Jesus in his third — and most graphic — prediction of his Passion (Mt 20:19; Mk 10:34; Lk 18:33). As for St. John, the bare fact of scourging is simply stated. He is not an eyewitness (as he will be at the crucifixion), yet he implies its singular position in the Passion as being, as it were, an intermediate conclusion to Jesus's trial: on the one hand, it shows him as already doomed; on the other hand, it shows him as giving his people one more chance to reconsider him — his grandeur and his humiliation — before they render a final judgment.

And so we reconsider him now. The evidence of a merciless flogging is imprinted on the Holy Shroud. We have but to see the marks: the crisscrossed furrows of blood across his back, front, and limbs. The marks themselves are silent — as he was silent then. But his Heart, whence came the blood, is speaking — as in Gethsemane — to his Father: Abba!

This is his response to what they — what we — did to him.

How long did the scourging last? Not as long as his consciousness of it.

SEQUEL TO THE SCOURGING

For our sake [God] made [Jesus] to be
sin, who knew no sin... (2 Cor 5:21)

HOWEVER long the ordeal lasted, Our Lord's consciousness outlasted it. But how can we fathom his feelings as, at last unfettered, he slumps to the floor at the foot of the pillar — a quivering mass of lacerated flesh and blood.

Here at last is the literal fulfillment of Isaiah's "Fifth Gospel": his description of the Suffering Servant of Yahweh.

> "... he had no form or majesty that we should look at him, nothing in his appearance that we should desire him.... He was despised and rejected by others; a man of sorrows and acquainted with infirmity; and as one from whom others hide their faces; he was despised and we held him of no account. Surely he has borne our infirmities and carried our diseases; yet we accounted him stricken, struck down by God, and afflicted. But he was wounded for our transgressions, crushed for our iniquities; upon him was the punishment that made us whole, and by his stripes we are healed." (Is 53:2–5)

The scourging was essentially the sign — the "sacrament" — of our imprinting of our sins on every member of his Body, so that now he is more recognizable as a worm than as a man (cf. Ps 21/22:6). It was, more graphically, our beating our sins into his Body — in such wise that he was now "made sin" for us, as St. Paul actually describes him.

Only thus laden with our sins could he go on with his Passion to the very end (cf. Jn 13:1) — which will be his Cross, where he, with our sins within him, will be killed.

THE MYSTERY OF THE
SCOURGING AT THE PILLAR

*Hail Mary, full of grace, the Lord is with
thee, blessed art thou among women, and
blessed is the fruit of thy womb, Jesus.*

ONCE more, as in the First Mystery of Christ's
Passion, Our Lady is absent. And her absence is
perhaps the more noticeable because of the presence
of so many others. This Second Mystery has been a
veritable procession: Annas, Caiaphas, Peter (yes, Peter
in the very midst), Pilate, Herod, Barabbas — not to
mention the nameless others: the guard who first hit
him, the servant girl, the amateur crew of spitters, and
the professional crew of floggers.

Where was there the least trace of pity? Of merest
decency? (There will be some decency and pity later,
mostly — if not all — from women: Pilate's wife, the
women on the Via Dolorosa, and that Woman blessed
among all. But this comes only later.)

Just as in the previous mysteries of the night before,
so now on this Good Friday morning Our Lady is simply fulfilling — as always — the will of her Son. From
her little chamber near the Cenacle on Mount Sion,
she awaits the call of the Beloved (cf. Cant 3:1). If he
chooses for now to hide his face from her, she remembers this happening before. In sorrow did she seek him
in this same Holy City.

This time, when he calls her — as surely he will —
their sinless sorrows will be made one in the final Sacrifice. But until then, she will wait.

*Holy Mary, Mother of God,
pray for us sinners, now and
at the hour of our death.
Amen.*

THE THIRD
SORROWFUL MYSTERY

✝

OUR BLESSED LORD IS
CROWNED WITH THORNS

THE PRAETORIUM

. . . the soldiers led [Jesus] away inside the palace
(that is, the Praetorium); and they called
together the whole battalion. (Mk 15:16)

WHAT now follows the Mystery of our Lord's scourging is a Mystery that, in the eyes of three of the Evangelists (St. Luke is silent here), quite literally crowns this central moment of the Sacred Passion: Our Lord's crowning with thorns.

We are told that he was now "led"; might that not really mean that they dragged him? Job with all his loathsome sores was surely a less ghastly sight. Limp and pallid, with all his wounds aflame, he at best hobbled along, once more manacled and clad with but a dingy cloth about his loins, up the steep steps to the courtyard above.

The fresh air of late morning is hardly a boon, following that awful hour in the dungeon. What normally would be bracing must have induced a chill, and the outdoor brightness must have hurt his eyes. Oh, if only for a moment he could simply rest.

But no, Jesus is shoved into the courtyard and set down on a backless bench in its center. All around him gathers the cohort: not an elite corps of imperial guards dressed for parade, but a nondescript company of thuggish mercenaries on garrison duty. The dregs of the provinces, they grunt a witless mix of barbarous Greek as they size up the scene.

Then, whether by some conniving hints from the governor or by some spontaneous impulse from the ranks, a crude pantomime, set on this back stage in mid-Jerusalem on this late Good Friday morning, begins to unfold.

THE CROWNING WITH THORNS

*And they clothed him in a purple cloak, and plaiting
a crown of thorns they put it on him. (Mk 15:17)*

WHAT unfolds now may be called the centerpiece of the Passion, just as it is the central Mystery of the Rosary: Our Lord being crowned with thorns. Whether on the spur of the moment or on a stratagem prearranged, the "soldiers" (we are given no names) come forward with a "crown" woven from some dried out sprigs of brushwood used for kindling a fire.

The sprigs have thorns—long, sturdy, and sharp. If the whips used in the scourging were bludgeons for scouring and mashing the body, the thorns are needles for incising and penetrating the head. His head had been spared the scourging; now it is its turn.

Using heavy leather gauntlets, the soldiers press the crown into place, straight across the forehead and around the base of the skull. It is not the neat circlet that is usually portrayed; rather it is a helmet, ill-shaped and bulky. The plaited sprigs stand out from the scalp, but the thorns—ah, they find their mark! Fresh blood spurts from scores of tiny incisions and streams down his face and neck.

Accompanying the crown on his head are a reed in his bound hands and a robe thrown across his shoulders and draping his naked body. It is a scarlet robe, so it brightens the drying blood from the flogging and matches the new glistening blood dripping from his head. What a sight! Even Isaiah's stark vision falls short of this.

What have they done to You, Lord Jesus?

THE MOCKERY

And they began to salute him, "Hail, King of the Jews!" And they struck his head with a reed, and spat upon him, and they knelt down in homage to him. (Mk 15:18–19)

THE first and ostensible object of this pantomime was to make Jesus so pitiable a creature that the crowd outside the governor's palace would say in effect: "All right, we are satisfied. This poor Galilean fanatic has had it; let him go. Whipped cur that he is, what's his life to us? Why, we Jews are with you Gentiles in seeing through his fakery. You've made a fool of him. Now finish your sport with him and let him go!"

Pilate's little plan will surely work. Besides rescuing him from committing judicial murder, it will humiliate these spiteful Jews, forcing them to admit that this Jesus, over whom they froth with envy (cf. Mt 27:18), is no threat to anyone. So get on with it, soldiers! Mock him well!

Our Lord had been proclaimed a king at his birth by certain wise men representing the Gentile world. Now a new set of representatives will repeal that proclamation by making it a joke. They cap their mockery by sticking in his bound hands a reed for a scepter and beating his head with it.

And as for his head, his crown of thorns, looking like an oversized bird's nest upside down, is all that is needed to tell the mob outside — and the world beyond — that this Jesus of Nazareth is a nobody: the butt of ridicule, a throwaway.

Yes, this is the world's first line of defense against Our Lord Jesus Christ. This is the world's answer to him: laughing in his face.

THE HATRED

Pilate went out again, and said to them, "Behold,
I am bringing him out to you, that you may know
that I find no crime in him." (Jn 19:4)

JESUS is led out on the balcony of the governor's palace. But Pilate's cruel calculation has misfired. After a
moment of stunned silence, the roar resumes: "Crucify
him! Kill him!"

The governor is clearly shaken, his truculent self-
confidence has vanished; his certitude that there are no
certitudes stands challenged. Why, this rabble has bested
him! And not just him personally but the whole sophis-
ticated system he represents: the worldly wisdom that
would make everything "negotiable." The cultivated
qualities of tolerance and wit are lost on this mob; all
they can appreciate is raw power stoked by raw emotion.

So Pilate's perverted pity only compounds the pitiless
fury of the people: Christ's own chosen people demanding that he die.

St. Paul may have had this standoff in mind when he
wrote to his Corinthians about the contrasting attitudes
of Jew and Gentile regarding Christ: "We preach Christ
crucified, a scandal to Jews and foolishness to Gentiles"
(1 Cor 1:23).

Which inflicts on Jesus the greater pain? To be dismissed with derision or to be hounded with hate? Jesus
crowned with thorns is at once a fool to the pagan for-
eigners who laugh at him, and a threat to his own people
who hiss at him. Which is worse?

Ridicule rejects wisdom; hatred rejects love. Either
is enough to break a man's spirit — but both! Yes, Jesus
crowned with thorns had both — and has both still (cf.
Jn 7:7; 15–18; 24–25).

Is there anyone out there who will, beyond all folly,
take him seriously? And, beyond all scandal, love him?

MARY'S ENTRANCE
INTO THE PASSION

Hark! My Beloved is knocking. "Open to me, . . .
my love, my dove, my perfect one; for my head is
wet with dew, my locks with the drops of the night."
. . . I opened to my Beloved, but my Beloved had
turned and gone. My soul failed me when he spoke.
I sought him, but found him not. (Cant 5:2, 6)

"IS there anyone who will take me seriously? Anyone who will love me?" These questions may well have been Our Lord's in that hour. After all, he's human! Still human, even after his humanity (not to mention his divinity) has been beaten out of him.

And so, through the blood and spittle, his eyes scan the crowd. And there, at the far edge of it, against a wall enclosing the great square, he sees what for any other would be but a speck; but for him it is everything! It is his Mother.

Oh yes, there are some whom he recognizes — the old man cured at the pool, the young man born blind but now seeing, and probably his dear Magdalen and John, accompanying Our Lady. But these scattered souls — can they really see him? At this moment they are too stunned to do anything but stare; their souls, scarred by whatever sins, are unable yet really to see! Only when he will be "lifted up" will they recognize him (cf. Jn 8:28).

But she, the one sinless one, recognizes him now! He must seem to be what she is in fact to him: so far removed and silent, in all that distance and din.

No matter. In this his "hour" — at this midpoint of his Passion — she finds him at last, as he has willed it: to behold him in her heart — to love him for us all.

ECCE HOMO

*...Jesus came out, wearing the crown of
thorns and the purple robe. Pilate said
to them, "Here is the man." (Jn 19:5)*

A T this same moment that Our Lady sees her Son
for the first time in the actuality of the Passion,
there occurs what we may call the official proclamation of the Passion to all mankind. For now the one
man in charge, Pontius Pilate, the stand-in for Caesar, the Lord of the World, strides to the balustrade,
takes hold of the scarlet robe, points to Jesus, and (to
the blare of trumpets?) shouts to the crowd below:
"Behold the Man!"

The sudden display of imperial splendor compounds
the contrast between the beaten Prisoner and his title.
Here, on the word of an emperor-god, is — "the Man."

The word used by Pilate is not *vir* but *homo* (St.
John's word is *anthropos*, but Pilate may well have used
his native language). If Caiaphas had unwittingly spoken prophecy before the Passion (cf. Jn 11:49–52), could
it not be that Pilate is now unwittingly doing the same?

For here is indeed "the Man": the New Adam,
though vestured still as the Old Adam, for he bears the
sins of all mankind in the wounds he is bearing now in
his mangled body.

After his death — to which he is soon going — another
prophecy will bid us look on him whom we have pierced
(cf. Jn 19:37). But now we must first look on him whom
we have wounded, and who thereby shares with us
the lot of our fallen humanity: weak and wretched,
prodigal and lost.

Yes, he is "the Man" — "Everyman." And the one
person who enabled him so to be, who gave him his
humanity, she is here beside us beholding him too.

ECCE MAGISTER

*...Jesus [said], "For this I was born, and for this
I have come into the world, to bear witness to the
truth. Everyone who is of the truth hears my voice."
Pilate said to him, "What is truth?" (Jn 18:37–38)*

SHORTLY before Pilate proclaimed Jesus as "the
Man," he had interrogated him privately and
became more convinced than ever that the charge
against him—that he was inciting rebellion against
Rome—was groundless. Jesus proved that his alleged
kingship was "not from this world." But that he was
in some other sense a King was the very truth for the
witnessing to which he had come into this world. "To
give witness to the truth": here was Our Lord's own
statement of his life's purpose.

Whether that witness is accepted or not, it stands—
and for it he will lay down his life. Already his life was
declared forfeit because of his affirmation that he was
"the Christ": the Anointed One, the Man from heaven.

What was blasphemy for the Jews is folly for the
pagans. "The truth" indeed! As Pilate scoffs, "What is
truth?"

Now on display on the balcony, "the Man" stands
before the crowd as he stood the previous night before
the Sanhedrin: he is the "Prophet": the "witness to
the truth," the Teacher. That had been his one consistent title all through his brief ministry (cf. Mt 23:1–10;
Mk 12:9; Lk 20:21; Jn 13:13). Here was indeed the first
meaning of his being "the Christ," from which all further—and deeper—meanings would flow.

The sophistry of Pilate (and his entourage) and the
fury of Caiaphas (and his colleagues) may reject this
Teacher, for they have free wills. But to his Mother
(and her few companions), there jostled in the crowd,
the truth is that he is the Truth—and his dying will
prove it.

ECCE REX

Now it was the day of Preparation of the Passover;
it was about the sixth hour. [Pilate] said to
the Jews, "Here is your king!" (Jn 19:14)

IF truth itself is unknown and unknowable, as Pilate averred, there are still some incidental truths that he does know: that mighty Rome and her emperor have nothing to fear from this peasant Galilean prophet, that these loathsome natives will deserve to have rubbed into them his being their Messiah-King, and that this whole sad day's affair will be soon forgotten.

So he puts Jesus once more on display, as (again with a flourish of trumpets?) he taunts the crowd: "Behold your king!" Yes, once more behold him! And what a vision it is!

By now what morning chill there was has vanished, and the near noonday sun has reopened his wounds. The terrible lesions all across his body have swollen, exuding a mucous liquid that almost glistens. What royal raiment! Outclassing the now shabby scarlet cloak that still limply clings. His fettered hands still hold the reed—his kingly scepter. And his throbbing head still wears the thorns—his imperial diadem.

"Come!" sneers Pilate; "kneel before him, you Jews! Acclaim him with 'Hosannas!' for he is your King!"

Our Lord had said that his kingdom was not "from here," but that "hereafter" it would be seen for what it always was and is and will be forever. It is not a wholly invisible kingdom, then, nor will it ever be. And because it is visible we can see him—and see him, indeed, as King.

But right now, on this first Good Friday, only one person does see him thus: his sinless Mother.

ECCE SACERDOS

Although he was a Son, he learned obedience
through what he suffered; and being made perfect
he became the source of eternal salvation to all who
obey him, being designated by God a high priest
after the order of Melchizedek. (Heb 5:8–10)

JESUS crowned with thorns, at once laughed at for
his folly and hated for his claims, is, at the midpoint
of his Passion, indeed the Anointed One: the Messiah,
the Christ. This title becomes his very Person, for it
means that he is, by inheritance and by merit, both
Teacher and King. As Prophet (or Teacher) he claims
our minds, all truth is his, and if we are to be in the
truth, we too must be his (cf. 2 Cor 10:5).

And as King (or Shepherd) he claims our wills: all
goodness is his, and if we are to be in goodness, we must
likewise be his. But then, if we are thus the disciples of
Christ the Teacher and subjects of Christ the King, what
final purpose is served by our belonging totally to him?
What is our ultimate destiny as Christians?

Is it not to become holy, that is, one with God the
Father, in the grace of our adopted sonship? Christ
teaches and governs us only in order to sanctify us: our
minds and wills made over to God only in order to have
our entire selves "divinized" through our incorporation
into the one Mediator (or Priest) between God and man,
the Man Christ Jesus (1 Tim 2:5).

So he stands before us now, robed in the Blood of his
Passion, which is indeed the true vesture of his Priesthood. With Our Lady, we behold him as he now proceeds to accomplish what he had already sacramental-
ized the night before at the Supper: the Sacrifice of his
life for the salvation and sanctification of all mankind.

THE MYSTERY OF THE CROWNING WITH THORNS

Hail Mary, full of grace, the Lord is with thee, blessed art thou among women, and blessed is the fruit of thy womb, Jesus.

IT was as crowned with thorns that Our Lord in his Passion was first seen by his Mother. They will not meet again until later, but that first mutual glimpse, across the vast square outside the governor's palace and with a teeming mass of humanity between them, will remain forever in Mary's memory (cf. Lk 2:51).

For this is the first time that she saw the actual fulfillment of the prophecies — Isaiah's in the Old Testament and Simeon's in the New — concerning her Son as the Suffering Servant and the Man of Sorrows, as the Sign of Contradiction and the Fall of many in Israel.

The ultimate fulfillment has not yet arrived, so the sword has not yet plunged to its destined depth. Yet even now she stands beside us as the closest witness to Christ — and therefore Queen of Martyrs. She directs our vision to him as to our Head — a Head circled with thorns.

Here in this central Mystery of the Rosary, as far from its beginning as from its end, our Hail Marys may sometimes seem more like thorns than roses — so disjointed and distracted, so weary and weak. But no matter. She presses them to her heart, good Mother that she is. And in her pain our own is lost.

Holy Mary, Mother of God, pray for us sinners, now and at the hour of our death. Amen.

THE FOURTH
SORROWFUL MYSTERY

✠

OUR BLESSED LORD
CARRIES HIS CROSS

THE DEATH SENTENCE

*... [Pilate] took water and washed his hands before
the crowd, saying, "I am innocent of this righteous
man's blood; see to it yourselves."... Then he
delivered him to be crucified. (Mt 27:24, 26)*

THE middle act in the five-act drama of the Passion,
the act that ended with Pilate's prophetic proclamation, "Behold the Man!" leads directly to the climax
of the whole drama: the death of Jesus Christ. For there
now takes place the one act of will—the decision made
by a single person—which will effect that result.

Pontius Pilate—and neither Caiaphas before him
nor Longinus after him—is the one person who effectively decided that Our Lord should die. That is why, no
doubt, only Pilate's name occurs in the Creed. The only
other human person named there is the Virgin Mary,
for she is the one person who effectively decided that
he should live. Both these persons stand there now at
this high noon of the Passion, far apart but both facing
Jesus, as his death sentence is pronounced.

This scene evokes that of the first death sentence of
all, when in Eden God decreed that Adam and Eve must
die. Ever since then, all their children, by the fact of
their having been born in their original sin, must live
their whole lives on death row, awaiting the execution
of God's justice—and mercy.

Yes, mercy—for now Our Lord joins all his brothers
and sisters by his free submission to death: "No one
takes my life from me; I lay it down of my own accord"
(Jn 10:18). Yes, mercy! For Pilate's will is used by God
to effect his will: the real cleansing of our sins in the
Blood of Christ.

THE CROSS

[Jesus] went out, bearing his own cross, to
the place called the skull, which is called
in Hebrew Golgotha. (Jn 19:17)

ONCE in the hands of the executioners authorized
by Pilate, Our Lord is given back his clothes: on
his way to death he would wear the seamless robe, noted
so carefully by St. John (cf. Jn 19:23). Then, in the inner
courtyard of the governor's palace, he is given the chief
instrument of his execution, to be carried by him to his
death: his Cross.

Imagine the scene left undescribed by the Gospels.
Death by crucifixion was common enough in the
Roman world, for it was how rebellious slaves and felo-
nious riffraff were disposed of. Two raw wooden planks,
stout enough to support a man nailed to them, to make
a spectacle of him while he writhes in lingering agony
until dead — such was the *crux horribilis*, providing the
cheapest and most efficient, the most humiliating and
painful capital punishment known to man.

What were the sentiments of the Heart of Jesus at this
moment of his first contact with his Cross? "I have a
baptism wherewith I am to be baptized, and how I am
impatient until it is accomplished!" (Lk 12:50). It was
for this that he had come down from heaven and had
taken to himself our sinful nature: to accomplish his
"Passion" — his passing over from sin to justice, from
death to life.

His Cross is therefore not a dead end of ignominy but
a springboard of liberation. By means of the Cross he
will "rebound" into heaven, while carrying with him
to his Father a redeemed humanity. Kneeling on the
cobblestones, Jesus kisses the wood of the Cross — the
wood of the very Tree of Life in Paradise.

THE FIRST FALL OF JESUS
UNDER THE CROSS

If any man would come after me, let him deny himself
and take up his cross and follow me. (Mk 8:34)

THE Via Dolorosa leads down into the city from the Temple Mount. Along this narrow way hemmed in by houses and the jostling press of a people curious and spiteful by turns, Our Lord carries the wood upon which he will die. Like the street, uneven and mean, so too is the wood weighing heavy on his lacerated shoulders. With a carpenter's eye and touch, he knows well the burden he carries: its inertia, its dumbness, its dead weight.

How utterly removed from him now are the sweet memories of that carpenter shop in Nazareth, or of those refreshing glens along the byways of Galilee. Even the cool moonlit groves of Gethsemane are gone. Now there is but the raucous noises and smells of a dirty street — and the pitiless press of his Cross.

At some point early on his journey, Jesus stumbles on a stone and falls. His Cross crashes earthward and pins him under its weight. His tunic, already bloodstained from his sweat the night before, is now besmeared with muck. His face is in the gutter, and he cannot move.

Perhaps it is the angel of the Agony who once more comes to him and whispers, "Arise and eat; you have yet a long way to go" (1 Kgs 19:7). So, with the food of his Father's will (cf. Jn 4:32, 34), he struggles to his knees and then to his feet, and plods on.

So too must we, if we are to follow him — carrying, as he clearly wills that we carry, our cross.

JESUS'S MEETING
WITH HIS MOTHER

*Oh all you that pass by the way, attend, and see if
there is any sorrow like to my sorrow... (Lam 1:12)*

ALTHOUGH Our Lady had already seen her Son
in his Passion — at that climactic moment when
he was proclaimed "the Man" by Pontius Pilate and
rejected as their King by his people, she had seen him
at a great distance, and she had no assurance that he
had seen her.

Now, some minutes later, they meet face to face —
and almost hand to hand. She was standing, with Mary
Magdalene and St. John, at a turn in the narrow street
as it rounded the last descent from Mount Moriah and
headed west across the slowly rising stretch toward the
city gate and Golgotha. It was at this last level place
along the Via Dolorosa (still marked by the tiny foot-
prints in mosaic enshrined amidst the traffic of that
busy street) that the angels arranged this penultimate
rendezvous of Mother and Son.

Now that she sees him clearly, she is all the more
appalled at what he has suffered. She reaches out to
touch him, but so transfixed is she with sorrow that
nothing happens but an exchange of looks. Beyond all
words, she knows to perfection the paradox of compas-
sion: how one's "suffering with" at once alleviates and
compounds the suffering of the other.

Indeed, what sorrow can compare with her sorrow
now? All the woes of her people now weigh on this
one virgin daughter of Israel, on this one widowed
mother of the Messiah. And none knows this more
keenly than Jesus, as he bears his Mother's grief as his
sweetest Cross.

SIMON THE CYRENNEAN

And [the soldiers] compelled a passer-by,
Simon of Cyrene, who was coming in from
the country, the father of Alexander and
Rufus, to carry his Cross. (Mk 15:21)

THERE is no mention in the Gospels of Our Lord's meeting his Mother on the Via Dolorosa. That was left to the tradition of the *sensus fidelium*. What *is* mentioned by all three Synoptics is Our Lord's meeting a North African stranger whom the soldiers guarding Jesus constrained to carry his Cross.

St. John does not mention this, perhaps to remove the unwarranted conclusion that Jesus did not therefore do what he had clearly implied when he summoned whoever would follow him to carry their crosses too. It would seem that Our Lord was so affected by the sight of his Mother that the soldiers sensed a need for someone to help him — that our carrying our crosses would actually help him to carry his.

What an appropriate symbol of the solidarity that Our Lord intends to have with his disciples! He intends that we form one body with him, that our own individual cross (which indeed it is!) form one cross with his. And that our helping him (which, by his will is really such) is but the complementary reality of his helping us — for his weakness is really our strength (cf. 1 Cor 1:25; 2 Cor 12:9–10).

And how appropriate that the individual person chosen to represent us all should be this Paschal pilgrim from distant Cyrene. He did not volunteer for this task; he was drafted — no doubt upsetting his holiday plans. But what may well have been resented at first came later to be the best and greatest hour of this Simon — who may well have become the first Christian layman!

VERONICA

... it is the God who said, "Let light shine out of darkness," who has shone in our hearts to give the light of the knowledge of the glory of God in the face of Christ Jesus. (2 Cor 3:6)

AT the midpoint of the Via Dolorosa, at its lowest and narrowest stretch before its slow incline upwards to the city wall (the site marked today by a tiny hospice of the Little Sisters of Jesus), tradition has it that a woman named Veronica offered Jesus her veil as a towel wherewith to wipe his face. Reminiscent of the ministrations of the Magdalene (and, long before, of the kisses of his Mother), this womanly gesture so touched the Heart of Jesus that then and there he bequeathed to her, and through her to all of us, a miraculous image — a veritable photograph — of his Holy Face.

The countless reproductions of this sacred image show, in varying degrees of similitude, the reality that was the Man named Jesus on that first Good Friday, and ever since. The forehead, the nose and cheeks, the chin, are indeed the features of the "most beautiful of the sons of men." And the blood and the sweat, the spittle and the mire, and the very disfigurations from his being scourged and crowned with thorns, only enhance the majesty of his patience and the glory of his humility.

But it is the eyes, whether open or shut, that hold us. Before we behold him whom we have pierced (cf. Jn 19:37; Rev 1:7), he already beholds us. Yes, even before he reaches the high hill of Calvary, even while still struggling through the city streets, he beholds — me.

THE SECOND FALL

If any man would come after me, let him deny himself,
and take up his cross daily and follow me. (Lk 9:23)

THE traditional Seventh Station on the Way of the Cross is a mystery unique in the great series of mysteries that is the Passion of Our Lord. It seems at first a mere repetition of the Third Station: Jesus falls once more under his Cross.

But whereas the first fall occurred very shortly after he began his journey to Calvary, and could therefore be ascribed to his unfamiliarity with his burden, now with more than half of his journey finished, it could be said that Jesus in his humanity has learned all too intimately the breadth and depth of his Cross.

Whereas the first fall resulted from all that had previously been done to him — the treasons and the taunts, the lashes and the thorns — all of which had so weakened him as almost to preclude his carrying his Cross at all, this second fall resulted not so much from his antecedent weakness as from his present failure — his failure to "measure up" to his Cross.

And why was this so? That he might identify by firsthand experience with our failure: our failure in carrying our cross "daily." No longer our mere weakness in accepting what has been given us, but now our failure in following through with what we had chosen: our failure in our intention to "stay the course."

We see Our Lord flat on his face beneath his Cross because he saw us there first, flat under ours. The last and greatest pride of all to be overcome is pride in carrying our cross.

THE DAUGHTERS OF JERUSALEM

*... there followed him a great multitude of people,
and of women who bewailed and lamented him.
But Jesus turning to them said, "Daughters of
Jerusalem, do not weep for me, but for yourselves
and for your children." (Lk 23:27–28)*

A S Our Lord, staggering from his second fall,
approaches the city gate, there awaits him a group
of women with their infants in their arms. Sharply
limned by the noonday sun against the backdrop of
the western wall, they form, as it were, the chorus of a
classic tragedy, their ululations echoing the immemorial
woes of Israel.

What memories this must have evoked for Jesus — the
widowed mother in Galilee weeping at the funeral of
her only son, and Jesus telling her not to weep and rais-
ing him to life (Lk 7:12–15). Or again, his own weeping
over Jerusalem for her not knowing the time of her
visitation (Lk 19:41–44).

Yes, women's tears — and his tears too because of
them — for the sorrows of the world, and for the sins
that from the beginning had caused them to flow. And so,
from the brimming pity of his Heart, he speaks to them
with Scriptural pathos and poignancy (cf. Hos 10:8).

Yes, all of us are present in his Passion: his suffering
with us and our suffering with him, in a suffering that,
once senseless and barren, now has meaning and fecun-
dity. For now, with our tears mingled with his, the dry
wood that was his Cross — and ours — will spring to life.

And once beyond the walled emptiness of this earthly
city and planted on the hill of Calvary, it will become
the green wood with fruit for food and leaves for healing (cf. Ez 47:12), the nurturing Vine and the Tree of
Life in Paradise.

THE ARRIVAL AT CALVARY

*...Jesus also suffered outside the gate in order
to sanctify the people through his own blood.
Therefore let us go forth to him outside the
camp, bearing abuse for him. (Heb 13:12–13)*

OUTSIDE the city gate toward the west, an out-cropping of rock called Golgotha served as a place
of refuse, where criminals were executed and garbage
was dumped. While the hot midday sun makes the place
more unsavory than usual, the bone-tired Prisoner
slowly wends his way through the filth, and, following
the orders of the guard, he lays down his Cross.

He lays it down gently; then he kneels beside it and
kisses the ground. This is the Ninth Station: the third
and final fall. Unlike the second fall, as the second was
unlike the first, this final mystery of the Way of the
Cross is softly anticlimactic. The once-wailing women
and the noisy city traffic and the curious holiday crowds
seem strangely muted, as though a theater audience
were quieting for a drama about to begin.

Meanwhile, on the slight eminence of the hill, Our
Lord is allowed by the soldiers to pause a moment
before the execution begins. Before they strip him of
his clothes and nail him to the Cross, he prepares for
this overture to the final act of his Passion by an act of
humility—whereby, for the last time in his mortal life,
he will be face to face with the solid earth.

He kisses the wood of his Cross and the rocky dirt
in which it will be planted. It is, as it were, a liturgical
prostration before he ascends the steps of the altar of
sacrifice. The next time he touches ground, he will be
a corpse.

THE MYSTERY OF THE
CARRYING OF THE CROSS

Hail Mary, full of grace, the Lord is with thee, blessed art thou among women, and blessed is the fruit of thy womb, Jesus.

OF all the twenty Mysteries of the Rosary, the Fourth Sorrowful Mystery may perhaps be the most familiar to devout Catholics, thanks to the popular devotion that historically paralleled that of the Rosary, and that in almost every church building of the Roman rite throughout the world the faithful invariably see gracing its walls: the fourteen Stations of the Way of the Cross.

The other Mysteries are events; this Mystery is a "career," in a sense the entire lifetime of the faithful Christian, one and all. Our Lord himself described his discipleship as the carrying of a cross (cf. Mt 10:38; 16:24; Mk 8:34; Lk 9:23; 14:27).

From our baptism's commitment to die with Christ Crucified, to our burial with him in expectation of the Resurrection, the Christian life from end to end is signed with the Sign of the Cross.

The fixed and central reality that is the Cross is, however, a moving, a "progressive" one as well. Each Christian's cross is unique, and each uniqueness has its variations and vicissitudes, its words and its silences, its companionships and its loneliness, its falls and its rising to begin again. The Way of the Cross is indeed the Way — the Way that alone is the Truth and the Life (cf. Jn 14:6).

Its ignominy is its glory, for it verifies the Christian as indeed it verifies Christ himself — binding as it does his surrender to his Father's will in Gethsemane with the consummation of that surrender on Golgotha. So for all the faithful — beginning with Our Lady, and potentially for all mankind — the Stations mark the milestones of the One True Life.

Holy Mary, Mother of God, pray for us sinners, now and at the hour of our death. Amen.

THE FIFTH
SORROWFUL MYSTERY

✠

THE CRUCIFIXION
OF OUR LORD

THE CRUCIFIXION

... they crucified him...
(*Mt 27:35; Mk 15:24; Lk 23:33; Jn 19:18*)

NOW begins the final Mystery of the Passion of Our Lord. All that has preceded it is prologue: the readying of the Victim for the last and definitive Act by which he is to save all mankind, making available to all the eternal life — by his dying.

The dying itself is an instantaneous act, which will not occur until three hours have passed. So, on this warm bright afternoon of the Preparation Day of the Pasch, the prologue is prolonged. It is the Father's will that all should see in broad daylight what men have done to him, "the Man." That this may be so, his Cross will now be in its intended place, upright and stationary, fixed in the earth, anchored in rock, on a hill named after a skull.

And the Man? He will be put on display, lifted up for all to see (cf. Jn 3:14; 8:28; 12:32).

Before the Cross is fixed in place, Jesus is fixed in his. His place is to be fixed to his Cross — nailed to it until he dies. First they strip him, so that he goes to his death totally despoiled, even of his clothes. Then they stretch out his arms and legs along the two beams of wood that are the Cross, and they secure them in place with iron spikes driven by hammer through his hands and feet.

Then, with him and his Cross as one dead weight, they heft him aloft. It is quickly done — almost as quickly as the time it took the four Evangelists to say it: "They crucified him."

THE FIRST WORD
FROM THE CROSS

Father, forgive them, for they know not what they do.
(Lk 23:34)

THE first of Our Lord's words following his crucifixion is recorded by St. Luke, and he seems to suggest that it was spoken immediately after the beginning of his three-hour agony on the Cross. It is now the "sixth hour"—midday: lunch hour for the milling throngs on a holiday weekend.

The execution of criminals, especially of one claiming to be "King of the Jews," is a public spectacle; and St. John notes that "many of the Jews" were there (Jn 19:20).

Jesus's words are addressed to his Father in prayer, but they are audible, meant to be heard—and recorded. It is the first audible prayer since Gethsemane, and it is the first explicit reference to forgiveness since the consecration of the chalice at the Last Supper (cf. Mt 26:28).

Jesus had referred to sin earlier in his Passion, but then it was in reference to guilt (cf. Jn 19:11). Now, precisely because of that guilt, he turns to his Father for its pardon—a pardon which only he, the all-knowing and all-loving God, can give.

And the reason for this pardon is that they do not know what they are doing (cf. 1 Cor 2:8). Some of them see Jesus as a harmless fanatic; others see him as a dangerous blasphemer. No one sees him as the Father's Son. For no one knows him but the Father (cf. Mt 11:27), and no one will know him until he is "lifted up" (Jn 8:28).

"So, Father"—he pleads—"now that I am lifted up on my Cross, let them know me! That knowing me, they may turn from their sins—to me!"

THE SECOND WORD
FROM THE CROSS

Amen, I say to thee: this day thou shalt be with me in Paradise.
(Lk 23:43)

"AND the people stood by, watching" (Lk 23:35). What impression on the part of the crowd is St. Luke conveying by this comment, following immediately as it does Our Lord's prayer to his Father for their pardon? It is, as it were, a microcosm of all mankind — a fulfillment of Christ's last public prophecy: "When the Son of Man comes in his glory . . . then he will sit on his glorious throne. Before him will be gathered all the nations . . ." (Mt 25:31–32).

They facing him and he facing them, the dialogue begins. He has prayed for their forgiveness, and his prayer is answered.

Now who will come forward to be forgiven? Out of all that crowd of sinners, only one act of contrition is recorded. One of the two criminals being executed with Jesus, one who with the other had till now been taunting Jesus to save them, suddenly falls silent. He looks across to this "King of the Jews" beside him — and out comes the simplest, most humble prayer in all the Scriptures: "Jesus, remember me when you come into your kingdom" (Lk 23:42).

Yes, here is the prophecy fulfilled, the end of history anticipated. "Then two men will be in the field, one is taken and one is left" (Mt 24:40). To the right and to the left they will be separated (cf. Mt 25:33).

The General Judgment but ratifies the Particular Judgment, the first revealed instance of which is this poignant dialogue between two dying men — between the King and his first canonized saint.

THE THIRD WORD
FROM THE CROSS

Woman, behold thy son. . . . Behold thy mother.
(Jn 19:26–27)

BY now an hour must have passed since Our Lord had been lifted up on his Cross. Those hating him seem satisfied that he can't (or won't?) come down from the Cross; those watching him out of mere curiosity are bored, as much by his silence as by the howls of the haters, and so begin to drift away.

Because of this, the soldiers on guard allow a handful of what look like faithful friends to approach the crosses. One in particular prompts their pity; it must be the mother of the One on the center cross. She comes closer, then stands there, looking up into the face of her Son. Their eyes meet—and through their eyes, their hearts. What a moment is this! It is at last "the hour" for which both have waited all their lives.

Mary has no words for this occasion, for none are needed. But Jesus has, for he must make an explicit twofold provision before he dies. He must provide for his disciples, now all scattered and shaken; they will need a mother as never before. So he bids her (whom he addresses once more as "Woman"—blessed above all women) to take John, standing by (and standing in for us all), as her own son.

And he must also provide for her. Widowed and bereft of her First-born Son, she must be cared for and cherished in a manner that would aspire to emulate his love for her—and her love for them.

THE FOURTH WORD
FROM THE CROSS

My God, my God, why hast thou abandoned me?
(Mt 27:46; Mk 15:34)

WE now approach the midpoint of that first "Tre Ore," which in turn is the high point of the Passion, and the center of human history. Our Lord is now utterly alone. His Mother and St. John and the Magdalene are still there and will be till the end, but they are now given away, no longer his very own.

He has indeed emptied himself (cf. Phil 2:7) — of all. Even their visibility is gone, for the weather has dramatically changed. The once bright afternoon has turned murky, an unearthly pall obscures the sun, and all nature is eerily silent.

Then, suddenly, out of that ghostly gloom comes a cry — a loud cry, we are told. *Eloi, Eloi, lama sabachthani!* The very words in the original Aramaic are etched forever in the world's memory.

For St. Matthew and St. Mark, they are the only words heard that afternoon from the Cross. They are the words of the Psalmist (Ps 21/22:1), but now they have a meaning of unutterable mystery — the mystery of the Son abandoned by his Father.

Suffering in his body the indescribable pain of crucifixion, Jesus now suffers in his soul a pain incomparably greater still. Here on Golgotha are the dregs of the chalice of Gethsemane. Willed by his Father's intolerable love, Jesus wills to make his own the feelings of Everyman the Sinner, who has in effect told God to leave him alone.

God respects his creature's free will: the Hound of heaven is called off, and the Man on the Cross is left to himself alone.

THE FIFTH WORD
FROM THE CROSS

I thirst. (Jn 19:28)

AFTER an hour or so of total silence in total darkness, the Man on the Cross once more speaks. But this time it is not a loud Biblical cry; rather, it is but a single word—*sitio*—a barely audible whisper. This word, ear-witnessed by St. John, is every bit as deep and mysterious as the word preceding it; it is its perfect complement.

On the one hand, it is so matter-of-fact and obvious. Drained by a relentless hemorrhage ever since Gethsemane, Our Lord's thirst that afternoon on Golgotha may well have been the most hellish of all his physical sufferings (cf. Lk 16:24). Yet, at the same time, this thirst goes far, far beyond the merely physical—just as it did on that distant afternoon beside a well in Samaria (cf. Jn 4:5–10).

It is "living water" that he is thinking of: the water welling up to eternal life that he had promised to give to all those who would come to him. "If anyone thirsts, let him come to me and drink.... Out of his heart shall flow rivers of living water" (Jn 7:37–38).

What he thirsts for is our thirst! This was the one enduring quest, the one unremitting plea of his Heart his whole life long: "Come to me...!" (Mt 11:25). Having turned to his Father in his abandonment, he now turns to us in his thirst. Will he die bereft of both? Or will he die, with his Father and with ourselves, together as one in the wellspring of his Heart?

THE SIXTH WORD
FROM THE CROSS

It is finished. (Jn 19:30)

IT is now nearing the "ninth hour" — three o'clock. The preternatural darkness had dismissed the crowd, and now only the faithful few with Our Lady stand by — while angelic spirits, good and evil, hover near. The evil? Yes, all around that hillock of the skull lay heaped the residue of ridicule and rejection, of trial and torture, that had been that night and day of the Passion.

Every sin that had ever been or that ever would be committed was there, piled up like a pyre about the Cross. Satan had done his worst; even his immeasurable energy for evil was exhausted. The body and soul of Jesus had been assaulted to a degree beyond comprehension.

There he hangs now, wrung-out and limp, almost phosphorescent in his pallor. He has absorbed — literally — every evil. "Made . . . to be sin who knew no sin" (2 Cor 5:21), before heaven and earth and under the earth.

But if the evil — raw evil, angelic and human — abounds there, the good superabounds (cf. Rom 5:20). Our Lord has taken all evil into himself, but — he still lives! For the good that is himself is unconquerable!

He will die on his terms and no other. Only when he has overfilled the mass of iniquity by the infinite mass of his love will his work be finished. But now, finally, everything has been done — "that the Scriptures might be fulfilled" (cf. Mt 26:56).

To the last detail, the one perfect life — fulfilling all others — approaches with majestic calm its finish.

THE SEVENTH WORD
FROM THE CROSS:
THE DEATH OF JESUS

Father, into thy hands I commend my spirit. (Lk 23:46)

JESUS has at last come to the consummation of that "hour" for which he had been sent by his Father and had come into the world. He came here to dwell among us—and to die. For only by so doing could he love us "to the end" (cf. Jn 13:1).

That "end," now that it has come, must have seemed to him to have come so quickly (cf. Mk 15:44). His whole earthly life was really so brief, and not in spite of but because of its incredible intensity—so very brief, now in retrospect, was his Passion. Just one night and one day—from the First Vespers of his Supper in the Cenacle to the Second Vespers of his Death on Calvary. It was hardly Promethean, this death of the Son of Man!

Yet it all happened exactly as willed by his Father. Much indeed was left wanting in his Passion (cf. Col 1:24); but that was so only because the Father wills that all his children now share with his First-born in the Love that makes Them one.

The guilt is gone, but the debt—the sweet debt of suffering love—remains until the end of time. To make that oneness with Christ Crucified a reality on the part of all mankind, Jesus now performs the last action—indeed the only action—of his Passion. He, the one Priest and Victim of Love, breathes back into his Father's hands his Spirit—his human soul and his divine Spirit together—in one total act of Love.

THE SACRED HEART AND THE PIETÀ

... one of the soldiers pierced his side with a
spear, and at once there came out blood and
water.... And ... scripture says, "They shall look
on him whom they have pierced." (Jn 19:34, 37)

JESUS now hangs dead upon his Cross. No sooner had he breathed his last than there occurred a groundswell of earthquake. The veil in the Temple behind him is riven, while before him the late afternoon sun recovers its light.

And in that unearthly light the Cross is revealed — with its sweet Burden — in perfect peace. *Dum volvitur mundus, Crux stat*. And now, in this setting, occurs the final and supreme revelation of Our Lord's Passion: the revelation of his Sacred Heart.

This is the divinely chosen symbol of what had caused his death. As anticipated in Gethsemane, before any hand had touched him, the Heart of Jesus ruptured from within. (Longinus's lance was but the instrument releasing a pent-up flood.) Christ's love for his Father and for us cannot be contained. From the moment of his death and forever, his Heart's love has a threefold witness: the Spirit, the water, and the blood (cf. 1 Jn 5:8).

This witness from the height of the Cross is now registered by earthly witnesses. There is the sworn witness of St. John (Jn 19:35), but before and after it there is the all-enveloping witness of Our Lady. Closest to Jesus at his death, as at his birth, is his Mother.

And after his death, the immemorial tradition of the Pietà has it that she received him into her arms. Taken down from the Cross by Joseph of Arimathea and John, the Body of Jesus reposes on his Mother's lap.

Thus is fulfilled the twofold prophecy: we behold him whom we have pierced, and we behold his mother beholding him — and us.

THE BURIAL OF JESUS

*...Joseph took the body, and wrapped it in a clean
linen shroud, and laid it in his own new tomb, which
he had hewn in the rock... (Mt 27:59–60)*

PERHAPS an hour has passed since the Body of
Jesus was taken down from the Cross. The quak-
ing earth has been stilled by the stillness of the sacred
Corpse: this dead Body is God himself!

Our Lady must now surrender It for burial. Joseph
of Arimathea and Nicodemus perform the preparation
with reverent haste, for the sun is near setting—and
with its setting the Sabbath rest begins.

Cool water bathes the ravages of the Passion, and
precious spices sweeten the rigor mortis that is now
enfolded in a clean linen shroud. Then the funeral
cortège winds its way down from the rocky hillock to
a nearby garden, where a newly opened grave is waiting.

The gravesite and the shroud are still with us. The
Holy Sepulcher is hardly recognizable after the vicissitudes of two millennia. But the contentious pieties
that have always surrounded this sacred spot—and still
do—must not obscure the simple historical fact: the
living God once died and was buried here.

As for the shroud, in spite of its vicissitudes (or perhaps rather helped by them!), its witness to the reality
of what happened on that first Good Friday is unmis-
takably clear. For it is, literally, a photograph of Jesus!

We see the same body and face that Our Lady saw.
The same unutterable sorrow, the same patience, the
same majesty. It is the providentially perfect souvenir
of the Passion, the very picture of the peace that was
Our Lord's earthly life—and never more so than when
he died and was buried.

THE MYSTERY OF
THE DEATH OF OUR LORD

*Hail Mary, full of grace, the Lord is with
thee, blessed art thou among women, and
blessed is the fruit of thy womb, Jesus.*

WITH the death and deposition and burial of Jesus,
the Sorrowful Mysteries of Our Lady's Rosary —
and her Seven Sorrows — are complete. As she retires
now to her little chamber near the Cenacle on Mount
Sion, let us join her at her invitation, and with her contemplate the mystery of what has happened through
these past twenty-four hours.

It is the "Mystery of Faith" that began with the Supper (at which she was present only in spirit), that continued with the Agony and the Scourging (the marks of
which she saw only later), that then found its crowning
symbols of thorns and Cross (which she indeed saw but
only in passing), and that finally was "lifted up" for all
to see — but for none more than herself, near enough to
touch, and to press to her heart when at last he came
down to her in death.

Yes, the Mystery of Faith is now sealed in the greater
Mystery of Love. A love at once totally human and
totally divine is poured out upon us from the pierced
Heart of Jesus, poured out through the heart of his
Mother — a heart also pierced, that thereby "thoughts
out of many hearts may be revealed" (Lk 2:35).

*Holy Mary, Mother of God,
pray for us sinners, now and
at the hour of our death.
Amen.*

THE
GLORIOUS
MYSTERIES

THE FIRST
GLORIOUS MYSTERY

✞

THE RESURRECTION

THE HOLY SEPULCHER

*In peace I will both lie down and sleep; for thou
alone, O Lord, makest me dwell in safety. (Ps 4:8)*

WHERE the Sorrowful Mysteries end, there the
Glorious Mysteries begin. As the Latin Vulgate
translates the Prophet Isaiah, "His sepulcher shall be
glorious" (Is 11:10). It is so because all the glories of
Christ and his Mother have their seedbed where the
Body of Jesus lay buried. "If [the seed] dies, it will bear
much fruit" (Jn 12:24).

Yes, this stage in the life of Jesus—the stage of his
death—is the ultimate state of his self-emptying. More
even than the act of his dying on the Cross, the state
of his being dead in the grave is the very bottom of
his abasement, his humiliation. For his Body was then
reduced to the state of mere chemicals.

Of course, that Body was still related essentially to
his human Soul, and—infinitely more—it was in its
very existence divine! Such was the humility of God on
that first Holy Saturday, and such was the basis—the
"launching pad"—for the glory of "the Man": the New
Adam, awaiting the first Easter Sunday.

What a gift of grace it is for us, who have lived in
a century—nay, a millennium—now dead, to have in
our presence the very image of the dead Body of Jesus
Christ! The Holy Shroud of Turin enables us to see what
only the adoring angels saw in the black death chamber
of Joseph's tomb.

While his Mother and his poor stunned disciples keep
the great Sabbath rest, there in the utter stillness of the
grave he lies: the living God, asleep.

LIMBO

. . . Christ . . . died for sins once for all, . . . that he might bring us to God, being put to death in the flesh but made alive in the spirit, in which he went and preached to the spirits in prison. . . (1 Pet 3:18–19)

ON that same first Holy Saturday in which the Sacred Body of Jesus rested in his grave, his Soul — as we are taught in the Apostles' Creed — "descended into hell." This was not the hell of the damned, the place our Lord often called "Gehenna" (Mt 5:22; 10:28; cf. Mk 9:43–48). Rather, it was what he called "Abraham's bosom," the "Sheol" of the just, where all those who had died in the Faith (if not the covenant) of Abraham awaited their salvation. It was a place of somber repose, visited by angels and removed as by a chasm from the place of fiery torment (cf. Lk 16:22–26).

Here he came, then, even farther down than his grave, "into the lower parts of the earth" (Eph 4:9). Awaking them from sleep, he will release them from their captivity and lift them with himself into Paradise.

See them all now as our Lord saw them on that great Sabbath day. There are Adam and Eve, who have waited the longest — his first human creatures and our first parents. There is the whole great procession of the Old Testament, from Genesis to John the Baptist. All of them now, patriarchs and prophets, priests and kings, parents and children — all see now what Abraham saw (cf. Jn 8:56) and rejoice.

But of all those present in that Sabbath jubilee, the one nearest and dearest to Jesus must be St. Joseph, that one "just man." Patiently he waits his turn, and then asks Jesus, "How is your Mother, Son?"

THE RESURRECTION
OF OUR LORD

... I delivered to you as of first importance what I also received ... that Christ rose from the dead on the third day, in accordance with the Scriptures. (1 Cor 15:3–4)

FRIDAY, Saturday, Sunday... it is now the third day. The Sabbath is past and a new week begins. As the original week began with God calling out of darkness, "Let there be light" (Gen 1:3), so on this first day of a new week a new creation begins, with God calling to himself the resurrection of his incarnate Son.

So from the sepulcher his body, and from Limbo his Soul, reunite in the one eternal existence of the Risen Christ. So on this first day of a new and unending week, Jesus enters into the New Creation.

Rather, he *is* the New Creation! In his very Person as God from God and Light from Light, his reunited humanity is newly begotten of his Father, in the Glory that is the Holy Spirit. Yes, his is Easter! "This is the Day the Lord has made; let us be glad and rejoice in it" (Ps 117/118:24)!

The Resurrection of Our Lord Jesus Christ from the dead is an event of history, in the sense that it occurred at a certain time and place in the "Old Creation" that began with Genesis. But it also transcends history, in the sense that its effect is a "New Creation": the new and Final Adam in the new and Eternal Covenant.

That is why the actual fact of Our Lord's Resurrection, although recorded in Sacred Scripture, is not described in it. Nor can it be! Nevertheless, in this third Hail Mary we contemplate the indescribable: we open our whole selves to the overwhelming reality of the Risen Christ, and in his light we see light (cf. Ps 35/36:9).

OUR LADY AND
THE RESURRECTION

*My beloved is mine and I am his; he pastures
his flock among the lilies. (Cant 2:16)*

ALTHOUGH it is not recorded — much less
described — in Sacred Scripture, it is the judgment
of Sacred Tradition that the very first person to see the
Risen Christ was Mary, his Mother. It is, upon reflection,
so obvious a fact that, speaking for the Tradition, St.
Ignatius in his *Spiritual Exercises** says it *is* in Scripture — for does not Scripture say, "Are you also without
understanding?" (Mt 15:16).

Just as Our Lady was the first to see her Son at
his birth (although that "firstness" is likewise not
recorded), so was she the first to see him newly begotten of the Father in his Resurrection. Indeed, she had
even more reason to be first at Easter than at Christmas,
for now — on her part — she who incomparably more
than anyone else had shared in his Passion, ought she
not be the first and foremost to share in his glory (cf.
2 Tim 2:11–12)?

But on his part too, this primacy must be hers. For,
as all the recorded apparitions make clear, the Risen
Christ was not at first all that recognizable. He had not
merely come back from the grave, he had gone forward into a new life — a life at once so splendid and so
simple that only the purest faith could grasp its reality.
"Blessed are the pure of heart, for they shall see God"
(Mt 5:8).

That faith was God's gift to her from the very beginning; he now simply crowns her Immaculate Conception. She sees her divine Son in a limpidity of faith
that, but for his will that she remain on earth, would
be heaven itself.

---

* Puhl, *The Spiritual Exercises of St. Ignatius*, no. 299.

THE ANGELS AND
THE RESURRECTION

*… an angel of the Lord descended from
heaven and came and rolled back the
stone, and sat upon it. (Mt 28:2)*

WERE the angels accompanying Our Lord when
he appeared to his blessed Mother? Just as at
Christmas, so here at Easter there is no mention of it.
Rather, as also at Christmas, the angels do participate in
the mystery, but they do so as the messengers that their
very name "angel" implies.

Our Lady needed no messenger, once Our Lord was
born — and risen. But all the other disciples do need
it; they must be shown the place where the mystery
occurred: the cave where he was born, and the cave
where he was buried. And who knows better these two
sacred places than the angels?

And so they are there, as the Gospels tell us. The
details vary: was there only one angel (as related by
Sts. Matthew and Mark)? Or were there two (as related
by Sts. Luke and John)? Or indeed were there angels as
such at all (Sts. Mark and Luke speak of "men")? Yet
the very confusion confirms the reality, for the women
are confused. They are "afraid" (just as the shepherds
were!), for they are in the presence of an astonishing
fact: they are seeking in a cemetery One who is alive
(cf. Lk 24:5)!

"Do not be afraid!" (Mt 28:5; Mk 16:6). This message
is for us — for all mankind caught in the toils of mor-
tality and unable of ourselves to recognize that which
is wholly alive. It takes a pure spirit from heaven to
see life aright and make it known. But the angels are
here on earth: "ascending and descending on the Son
of Man" (Jn 1:51).

MARY MAGDALENE

*Jesus said to her, "Mary." She turned and
said to him, "Rabboni!" (Jn 20:16)*

THE "confusion" in the Gospel records of the Resurrection regarding its details is the surest, sweetest
proof of their authenticity. Neither the number nor
even the identities of the angel messengers are clearly
stated. The same is true regarding the holy women to
whom the angels spoke.

Apart from Our Lady, who in her little room on
Mount Sion — close to the Cenacle where the Paschal
Mystery began on Thursday evening — remained walled
in light, her women companions were bustling about in
Sunday's pre-dawn darkness, attending by anticipation
to a corpse. Finally, there comes into this "confusion"
a point of light: the unmistakable personality of the
woman destined by Jesus to be the "apostle to the Apostles," the first formal human witness to the reality of
the Resurrection — Mary Magdalene.

Our Lord's appearance to her is one of the brightest
jewels of the New Testament. First of all, what could be
more significant than the fact that she had been a sinner
out of whom seven demons had been cast (cf. Mk 16:9)?

And then the circumstances of this encounter: the
initial shock of her seeing a dark empty grave, followed
by her tear-blurred sight of a seeming stranger, and
then the one word "Mary" that clears everything — as
instantaneously the dew-fresh garden becomes a glistening Paradise! Finally, the gentle admonition: the time
for embracing is not yet.

Heaven must wait, until the Good News is announced
to his brothers. Only then, in the House of his Father
and ours, will our ecstatic encounter be complete.

EMMAUS

*When he was at table with them, he took the bread and
blessed and broke it, to give to them. And their eyes
were opened, and they recognized him. (Lk 24:30–31)*

THE First Easter Sunday was indeed the Day that
the Lord has made (cf. Ps 117/118:24), but its celebration right then and there was more in heaven than
on earth. Apart from the first "Alleluias" by Our Lady
in her little chapel at midnight, and Mary Magdalene's
"Rabboni" in the garden of the sepulcher at dawn, "there
is no speech, nor are there words" (Ps 18/19:3) — only
the words of rapt contemplation echoing the awe of
the angels.

After the few whisperings and scurryings in its early
hours, most of the day is left silent in Scripture. The
only event that must have taken place was Our Lord's
appearance to St. Peter. Yes, Peter's confession is Easter's "high noon": the Church's first solemnly attested
memory of the Day of Days.

But even then, we do not hear of it until evening had
come, following an incident that only St. Luke tells us
of: the glorious "Second Vespers" of Easter — Emmaus!

On a country road and in a wayside tavern outside
Jerusalem that afternoon occurs a casual encounter
between two of the disciples and a Stranger. In this
simple setting, Our Lord reveals to the "rank and file"
of his Church the reality of the Resurrection. It is the
prototype of the Sunday Mass, which will sustain the
Church forever: the Scriptures opened in the Liturgy
of the Word, and the Bread broken in the Liturgy of
the Eucharist.

Only then will our hearts begin to glow; only then
will we recognize the Lord.

"MY LORD AND MY GOD!"

*Jesus said to [Thomas]: "Have you believed
because you have seen me? Blessed are those who
have not seen and yet believe." (Jn 20:29)*

IT was now the evening of the Day that the Lord
had made, and it was now the time that the officially
accredited witnesses of the Resurrection were at last to
see the Lord. Following Our Lady and the holy women,
St. Peter had already seen him, and on his word the
other Apostles believed.

But since all the rest of mankind to the end of time
were to believe with due certainty only on their col-
legial witness, the Apostles as a body had to see with
their eyes and touch with their hands the Body of the
Lord (cf. 1 Jn 1:1). And so that Sunday evening in the
Cenacle, they did just that. There in their very midst
he stood, while they in sheer wonder "disbelieved for
joy" (Lk 24:41).

Great things then happened. He breathed upon them
his Spirit: his peace and his pardon, by virtue of which
this Easter would reach to the whole world and never
end (cf. Jn 20:19–23). To symbolize this perpetuity, Our
Lord would use once more the weakness of men—his
men—to confirm them in his strength.

In a "little while" they will see him again, for his
Easter is more than a single natural day; it will be forever! And so on its Octave day, the following Sunday
foreshadowing eternity, he sees them again and they
see him again.

And in the person of St. Thomas, they touch him—in
his very Heart! At last all doubts are gone, for here in
their midst forever is their Lord and their God!

"IT IS THE LORD!"

That disciple whom Jesus loved said to Peter,
"It is the Lord!" (Jn 21:7)

WITH their first climactic affirmation of the absolute divinity of Jesus — their Lord and their God — the Apostles in the person of St. Thomas close the Easter Octave; as likewise the Apostles in the person of St. John close the book of the Gospels: ". . . these are written that you may believe that Jesus is the Son of God, and that believing you may have life in his name" (Jn 20:31).

But this same St. John adds a postscript: the Church's Easter is not merely a day nor even a week; it is a season — a lifetime! And so he records a "third time when Jesus was revealed to the disciples" (Jn 21:14): this time no longer in the Holy City but back home in Galilee, back in the workaday world of their ordinary lives. They once more are fishing in Peter's boat. After a nightlong catch of nothing, the dawn breaks over the springtime hills and a light mist skims the lake.

Suddenly, across the quiet waters comes a voice: a Stranger is on the shore addressing them. Of the seven men in the boat, only one recognizes the Stranger. John, "the disciple whom Jesus loved," says to Peter, "It is the Lord!" (Jn 21:7). Immediately Peter springs to action.

We know the sequel: this is the day when Peter becomes the pope! But this day's event begins with John (just as it will end with him!). It is his faith, quickened by the love of Jesus and Mary (who is now already in his care) that quickens in turn the faith of the Apostles.

This is indeed the Risen Lord — for seeing is believing. But even more, as he himself had told them, believing is seeing! (cf. Jn 20:29).

THE MYSTERY OF THE
RESURRECTION OF OUR LORD

*Hail Mary, full of grace, the Lord is with
thee, blessed are thou among women, and
blessed is the fruit of thy womb, Jesus.*

THE First Glorious Mystery has something almost unique among all the Mysteries of Our Lady's Rosary. Unlike the First and Second Sorrowful Mysteries in which she is certainly absent, and unlike the eleven other Mysteries in which she is conspicuously present, here in the Mystery of Our Lord's Resurrection she is present, but only hiddenly so. The only other Mystery comparable in this respect is the Third Sorrowful Mystery, where — as we may surmise — she is present, but only afar off. Here she is present, but she is so close to Jesus that she is lost in his light!

Far from having any regrets concerning this arrangement of things, we must strive to see its perfect fittingness. Our Lady is actually closer to Jesus in his Resurrection than she is even in his birth or in his death. Neither the Crib nor the Cross can ever be absent from her heart, but it is only and precisely because of his Resurrection that this is so!

What St. Paul said as applied to himself is even more applicable to Mary: ". . . even though we regard Christ from a human point of view, we regard him thus no longer" (2 Cor 5:16). And why is this so? Because, as he says elsewhere, "Set your minds on things that are above, not on things that are on earth. For you have died, and your life is hid with Christ in God. When Christ which is our life appears, then you also will appear with him in glory" (Col 3:2–3).

*Holy Mary, Mother of God,
pray for us sinners, now and
at the hour of our death.
Amen.*

THE SECOND
GLORIOUS MYSTERY

✠

THE ASCENSION

THE FORTY DAYS

*To [the Apostles Jesus] presented himself alive after his
Passion by many proofs, appearing to them during forty
days, and speaking of the Kingdom of God. (Acts 1:3)*

N OW begins that period in Our Lord's life which,
for all its brevity of forty days, is surely the most
fascinating, the most suited to our contemplation, precisely because it is the most mysterious. For here he is
now, even more than he was in his mortal life, at once
so magnificent in his majesty and so captivating in his
gentleness and lowliness of heart.

He is now both hidden and revealed, both already
in heaven and yet still on earth, both Lord of all and —
"only Jesus" (cf. Mt 17:8). It is almost as though he were
playing "hide and seek" with his disciples, in the win-
some, playful manner of unalloyed friendship and trust.

St. Ignatius summarizes the contemplative prayer by
which we join those first disciples in that first Easter
season in vernal Galilee. In the fifth and final Point of
his typical contemplation for the Fourth Week of the
Spiritual Exercises, he bids us "consider the office of
consoler that Christ Our Lord exercises, and to compare
it with the way in which friends are wont to console
each other."*

Thus he consoles Peter and each of his Apostles in
turn, and thus the holy women and all his "little flock"
(cf. Lk 12:32), to whom his Father will give the kingdom,
about which in these final colloquies he speaks to them.

Indeed, he is now more than ever the Good Shepherd, mindful of his little ones whom he calls by name
(cf. Jn 10:3) and carries in his arms (cf. Lk 15:5). Yes,
his scattered sheep (cf. Mk 14:22) are now once more
gathered, one by one, into his opened Heart.

---

* Puhl, *The Spiritual Exercises of St. Ignatius*, no. 224.

THE APOSTOLIC COMMISSION

...Jesus came and said to them, "All authority in heaven and on earth has been given to me. Go therefore and make disciples of all nations..." (Mt 28:18–19)

SOMETIME during those forty days—probably toward their end—our Risen Lord appointed a rendezvous with his Apostles on a mountain in Galilee. Was it Thabor? Or Carmel? Or some peak farther north toward Caesarea Philippi? In any event, it was to be a climax, a finale of the commission given him by his Father, which mission he was now formally to pass on to them. "As the Father has sent me, so I send you" (Jn 20:21). St. John records the equivalent as occurring on Easter Sunday itself. And now St. Matthew makes it the conclusion of his Gospel.

With the grandeur and matter-of-factness with which he dispels the last of their lingering doubts, Jesus begins by telling them that "all power in heaven and on earth" has been given to him (Mt 28:18). He then tells them that this power is theirs: to reach all men with all his teachings for all time to come. A threefold "allness"—in the name of the triune God.

Thus we have the formal mandate of Christ's Church—One, Holy, Catholic, and Apostolic—to teach, govern, and sanctify all mankind. Although only "the eleven disciples" are mentioned as present, for they are the formal recipients of this commission, it may well be that others were there too—perhaps the "five hundred brethren" mentioned by St. Paul (cf. 1 Cor 15:6).

If so, we can see here already a miniature of the Church, in a kind of "rehearsal" for Pentecost.

Already there is the interaction of "witness"—member with member in the one Body—moving toward "the measure of the stature of the fullness of Christ" (Eph 4:13).

OUR LORD'S FAREWELL
TO HIS DISCIPLES

*A little while and you will see me no more, and again
a little while and you will see me. (Jn 16:16)*

AFTER the great rendezvous in Galilee — the "Galilee of the Gentiles" so replete with memories for
Jesus and his little Galilean flock — there was, as St. Luke
(the only Gentile among the Evangelists) clearly states, a
return once more to Jerusalem. For only in the Holy City
of the Passion and the Resurrection could the Paschal
Mystery be completed, and only "from Jerusalem" could
the Mission to the whole world begin (cf. Lk 24:47).

So back they come — to the Cenacle, where it all
began on that Thursday evening six weeks before. See
them now once more in that "large upper room fur-
nished and ready" (Mk 14:15), ready with even more
poignant memories, for here is the only place where the
Master spoke explicitly of how he was to be remembered (cf. Lk 24:19).

It is in the context of the Last Supper, then, that we
are to remember Jesus. That is how St. John, who was
the closest to Jesus that night, remembered him. It is the
"hide-and-seek," the losing and finding, of the Risen
Christ and of his Eucharist — a theme that permeates
his Last Discourse. "I go to prepare a place for you.... I
will come again and will take you to myself, so that
where I am you may also be" (Jn 14:2–3).

"I will not leave you desolate; I will come to you. Yet
a little while and the world will see me no more, but
you will see me" (Jn 14:19). "I tell you the truth: it
is to your advantage that I go away, for if I do not go
away, the Paraclete will not come to you; but if I go, I
will send him to you" (Jn 16:7). "A little while and you
will see me no more; again a little while and you will
see me" (Jn 16:16).

Yes! We will see him — only in his Paschal Mystery.

THE ASCENSION
OF OUR LORD

... as they were looking on, he was lifted up, and
a cloud took him out of their sight. (Acts 1:9)

IT is on the Mount of Olives, at the foot of which is Gethsemane, that Our Lord takes leave of his disciples to return to his Father. It is the completion of the circle: "I came from the Father and have come into the world; again I am leaving the world, and going to the Father" (Jn 16:28).

His coming down from God to us is now completed by his going up from us to God. "He who descended is he who also ascended far above all the heavens, that he might fill all things" (Eph 4:10; cf. Phil 2:8–9).

The symmetry is perfect! On two Thursdays six weeks apart, the Paschal Mystery begins and ends. The whole Mystery is renewed daily in the Mass, but it is not a "renewal" that merely recurs; it is not circular but straight—straight as a sword, from heart to heart.

Our Lady is not mentioned by St. Luke as being present at the Ascension of her Son, any more than she is mentioned as being present at Pilate's proclamation of her Son as "the Man." However, only a "little while" later will she be mentioned by both Evangelists as being present both at the Cross and in the upper room awaiting Pentecost (cf. Jn 19:25; Acts 1:14).

As mothers' wombs enfold their children, so do their hearts encircle them all their life long. And in that circle, all their joys are sorrows, and all their sorrows are joys (cf. Jn 16:21). Such was Mary's heart encircling Jesus. But that circle was pierced by a sword—a sword straight from his Heart to hers, and from her heart to his.

"AT THE RIGHT HAND
OF THE FATHER"

*... the Lord Jesus ... was taken up into heaven, and
sat down at the right Hand of God. (Mk 16:19)*

THE "cloud" that St. Luke speaks of in his description of Our Lord's Ascension (Acts 1:9) has indeed taken him out of their sight and ours; only on the rarest of occasions has that veil been drawn aside (cf. Acts 7:55; 26:13).

For ordinarily, the light of Christ's presence in heaven is such that no one on this earth can see it and still live. What Moses had been told by Yahweh on the heights of Sinai, "You cannot see my face, for man shall not see me and live" (Ex 33:20), is confirmed by St. Paul speaking of Our Lord Jesus Christ as "[dwelling] in inaccessible light, whom no man has ever seen or can see" (1 Tim 6:16). This is because the Man Jesus is in his Person "God from God and Light from Light ... begotten not made, one in being with the Father."

The first essential truth of the Ascension is that its glory is not something "new" for Jesus. It is a divine glory; he had it with the Father before the world was made (cf. Jn 17:5). The absolute equality of Father and Son in Their mutual knowledge (cf. Mt 11:27) suggests a corresponding mutuality in Their being "side by side" (cf. Ps 109/110:1, 5).

Such is the traditional imagery used by the Church: Father and Son sitting together in the "Glory" that is Their Holy Spirit. Yet this is only an image that is less a vision than it is a veil. For this is the Holy of Holies, the Absolute, which in the Mystery of the Ascension we—with Our Lady and the Apostles—adore.

"THE FIRST-BORN"

He is the image of the invisible God, the
first-born of all creatures ... the first-born
from the dead. (Col 1:15, 18)

THE first essential truth, by which every other truth is validated, is the absolute divinity of Our Lord Jesus Christ. "True God from true God," he is with the Father and the Holy Spirit the only One who simply "is" (cf. Jn 8:58).

Now this first essential truth is "completed," as it were, by a second essential truth, which is itself "completed" by this Mystery of Christ's Ascension. And that is the truth of his absolute humanity — absolute in the sense that he is, as it were, "Everyman."

Yes, there, side-by-side with God, is a Man! And he is there by a twofold title: he is "the first-born of all creatures" and he is "the first-born from the dead." He, Jesus, is there beside his Father first by inheritance: "all things were created through him and for him" (Col 1:16; cf. Jn 1:3). And secondly, he is there by merit: "reconciling to himself all things ... by the blood of his Cross" (Col 1:20}.

He who was once "a worm and no man" (Ps 21/22:6) now gathers up into his humanity all creatures (even worms!) and brings them back to God.

In his Ascension, therefore, Our Lord is not simply there in repose. His presence in heaven is active: he is exercising his primacy by loving his Father, by praising him, by interceding for all his "brethren" in the eternal liturgy of his sacrifice (cf. Heb 7:25). That is why his Risen Body is still wounded. He, "the first-born from the dead," will effect the resurrection from death of all who believe and hope in him — when the "fullness" already won by his Paschal Mystery will be complete.

"LOOKING UP TO HEAVEN"

*... while they were gazing into heaven as he
went, behold, two men stood by them in white
robes, and said, "men of Galilee, why do you
stand looking into heaven?"* (*Acts 1:10–11*)

IN spite of the "cloud"—the veil of the sanctuary—
which hides from us now the vision of God and his
Christ, we still look up to heaven, and rightly so. St.
Paul says that, in a certain sense, we are actually seated
with Christ already in the heavenly places (cf. Eph 2:6)!

And because that is so, our "conversation" (to use the
word in the old English version) is already in heaven
(cf. Phil 3:20). We who are members of his Body by
our baptism and Holy Communion are not strangers to
heaven! Rather, we are strangers to earth (cf. 1 Pet 2:11).
Here we are in exile, still living in the Exodus where
our only habitation is a tent!

Our only home, therefore, is in the Promised Land
of heaven. Unbelievers may taunt us with our "pie in
the sky." We should thank them for reminding us to
keep our eyes on high, for only then—by a paradox of
Providence—will we escape the snares at our feet (cf.
Ps 24/25:15).

We will accomplish God's will on earth only if
we constantly refer to its accomplishment "as it is in
heaven." For there alone is the "house built by Wisdom" (Prov 9:1), built by the Master Carpenter, who
went ahead to prepare it for us (cf. Jn 14:2). And what a
house of unspeakable splendor it must be (cf. 1 Cor 2:9)!
Its "many mansions" (to use the Vulgate once more)
signify the multitude of fellow creatures, angelic and
human, in our Father's house; but their number is not
yet complete, for we are still missing.

What a family reunion it will be when at last we poor
prodigal pilgrims come home!

OUR LORD'S PROMISE TO RETURN

This Jesus, who was taken up from you into heaven, will come in the same way as you saw him go into heaven. (Acts 1:11)

THE two middle Articles of the Creed—the Sixth ("He ascended into heaven") and the Seventh ("from whence he shall come to judge...")—are separated by an indefinite span of time (*when* will he come?). However, not in spite of but because of that, they are closely united, as the angels (the "two men in white robes") reminded the Apostles.

Almost two millennia have now passed, yet for the Risen and Ascended Christ it is but "a little while" (Jn 16:16; cf. 2 Pet 3:8). In fact, he began to render judgment almost immediately after his entry into heaven, as St. Luke himself notes regarding St. Stephen (cf. Acts 7:56–60). Then began what Sacred Tradition calls the "Particular Judgment," which Our Lord makes for each and every person at the moment of death and which will culminate in the "General Judgment," when, at the end of time, all mankind will be gathered before him for their final public consignment to heaven or Hell (cf. Mt 25:46; Jn 5:28–29).

What should be our response to this awesome revelation awaiting us of Christ the Judge? Our Lord himself tells us, emphatically and often in his Gospel—it is in a sense the whole of his Gospel. St. Luke summarizes it well with these words of Jesus: ". . . look up and raise your heads, for your redemption is drawing near" (Lk 21:28).

Yes, this is the "Good News": Christ the Judge *is* Christ the Savior. "Yesterday, today, and forever" (Heb 13:8) he is the same one Jesus. Look up to him, stay close to him, and all will be well.

"REJOICING IN HOPE"

*... they worshiped him, and returned to
Jerusalem with great joy. (Lk 24:53)*

WITH these words, St. Luke concludes his Gospel,
his "first book" (Acts 1:1). They state the point of
departure for its sequel: his Acts of the Apostles. Yes, the
very first "act" of Our Lord's Apostles after his Ascension is neither one of sad resignation nor even of wistful
nostalgia; rather, it is one of rebounding gladness and
exuberant prayer—right there in the Temple where the
"first book" began (Lk 1:8–9).

Here, then, is the "bottom line": the theme of the
Good News threading its way through "all that Jesus
began to do and teach" (Acts 1:1), which the Apostles
remembered on that Thursday at high noon, and which
was to sustain them through all the days and weeks
and months and years and decades and centuries and
millennia to come—until this same Jesus will come "in
the same way [they] saw him go into heaven" (Acts 1:11).

In the Apostolic Tradition, this thread linking the
disciples' faith at the start with their love at the end is
called hope (cf. St. Paul on "these three" at 1 Cor 13:13).
Hope is the virtue of the "middle": the one essential
habit spanning the entire life of the Christian. For it
alone *is*, in the present time, our salvation.

Only by hope are we now "saved" (cf. Rom 8:28).
Hope is the combination of desire and confidence,
springing from faith and issuing in love—that is our life.

And accompanying it as its authenticating mark is
joy. "Rejoice in your hope" (Rom 12:12; echoed in Vatican II's *Gaudium et Spes*). To Jesus in heaven we lift up
our hearts—*sursum corda*! And behold! In our hope he
is here!

THE MYSTERY OF THE
ASCENSION OF OUR LORD

Hail Mary, full of grace, the Lord is with
thee, blessed art thou among women, and
blessed is the fruit of thy womb, Jesus.

SOMETIME shortly before his Passion, Our Lord had said, "If I am lifted up, I will draw all things to myself" (Jn 12:32). He had spoken of his being "lifted up" two times before (cf. Jn 3:14; 8:28), and in the context of his whole Gospel, St. John sees this being "lifted up" as the one single high-point of the earthly life of Jesus, verified equally in his Crucifixion and in his Ascension.

The two moments are ultimately but one, in the one integral Mystery of his Passover. Such is the way the Church has always seen her Lord: through the eyes of St. John and his Mother Mary, who were both present at both moments on both mountains: Calvary and Olivet.

In no other Mystery of the Rosary is our being "lifted up" to Jesus — and with Jesus — so paradoxical, so mysterious, so glorious! He is so far away, transcending the cosmos itself (cf. Eph 4:10); yet he is so near, as near as our very heartbeat and breathing.

The distance of his being "lifted up" is incalculably great, yet the power of his "drawing" is greater still. And how are we "drawn"? By hope! Here is our being "lifted up" to and with Jesus now — as mediated by her whom we invoke as "our life, our sweetness and our hope."

Holy Mary, Mother of God,
pray for us sinners, now and
at the hour of our death.
Amen.

THE THIRD
GLORIOUS MYSTERY

✠

THE DESCENT OF
THE HOLY SPIRIT

THE CENACLE

. . . when they entered [Jerusalem], they went up to
the upper room, where they were staying. (Acts 1:13)

THE "upper room" mentioned by St. Luke as the place where Our Lord's disciples gathered after his Ascension was probably the same "upper room" mentioned by him as the place of the Last Supper (cf. Lk 22:12). It might also have been part of the house later mentioned by him as belonging to Mary, the mother of John Mark (cf. Acts 12:12).

In any case, it must have been located in Jerusalem, and most likely in that quarter of the Holy City called Sion, west of the Temple Mount and south of the Holy Sepulcher. Here was the original city of David, and here to this day is his tower and his tomb.

Amid such memories, the disciples gathered — some hundred and twenty brethren (cf. Acts 1:15) — staying together at Our Lord's command, to await the coming of the Promise of the Father upon them (cf. Lk 24:49), with Peter as their head and with Mary the mother of Jesus as their heart (cf. Acts 1:14).

Memories and expectations, the past and the future, are here centered in this "upper room" where the Paschal Mystery will come full circle to its completion. The Passover of the Old Testament was fulfilled and the Passover of the New was begun in this Cenacle, with the institution of the Holy Eucharist.

Now this Passover will itself be completed with the coming of the Holy Spirit. Thus, what will be the salvation of all mankind and its completion in all time and space will begin in this Cenacle — with the birth of the One, Holy, Catholic, and Apostolic Church.

THE FIRST NOVENA

*All . . . with one accord devoted themselves
to prayer, together with the women and
Mary the Mother of Jesus. (Acts 1:14)*

OUR Lord's instruction to his disciples was that
they were to stay in the Holy City until they
were "clothed with power from on high." Only then,
"beginning from Jerusalem," were they to go forth to all
nations as his witnesses (cf. Lk 24:47–49). He did not
tell them how long a wait it would be until the Promise
of the Father would be fulfilled—first for the coming
of the Holy Spirit there in Jerusalem, and then for his
own coming again at the end of time.

In both waitings, they were to do what he had bade
his Apostles do on the eve of the Passion: "watch and
pray" (Mt 26:41; Lk 22:40). Before any action comes
prayer, and prayer is simply "watching" Jesus in communion with his Father in Their Spirit, and by this
"watching," entering into that same communion of the
Blessed Trinity. Only then could they go into the action
of their apostolic witness—in the Name of the Father
and of the Son and of the Holy Spirit.

These instructions were meant first and foremost for
the Twelve (which is why their number was restored
by the choice of St. Matthias), but not exclusively for
them. Ten times their number were there in the Cenacle,
for there was a little body of the faithful—men, women,
and children—as a miniature model of the Church,
awaiting the coming of its Soul.

With Our Lady—as on her Annunciation Day—they
watch and pray the First Novena. Come, Holy Spirit!

THE DESCENT OF
THE HOLY SPIRIT

... suddenly a sound came from heaven like
the rush of a mighty wind, and it filled all the
house where they were sitting. (Acts 2:2)

THEN "suddenly," we are told, it happened! It was nine o'clock on Sunday, the day after the seventh Sabbath of the seventh week after Passover — the same length of time that had elapsed between the Passover of Israel out of Egypt and their gathering at the foot of Mount Sinai, to receive through Moses the Covenant of Yahweh their God.

The same mighty wind that accompanied the theophany of that first "fiftieth day" in the desert of Sinai now fills that same upper room on the Mount of Sion where Our Lord had breathed upon his Apostles the Holy Spirit. The watching and praying that he had commanded of them has prepared them to receive his Spirit, that mysterious Breath of Life which will enable them to live anew (cf. Jn 3:6–8). "And they were all filled with the Holy Spirit" (Acts 2:4).

In the wind was fire from heaven — the fire that Our Lord had come to cast upon the earth (cf. Lk 12:49). From its core, as from a tornado, it now spread out to rest on the heads of each of the disciples. They all became, as it were, living candles!

The 120 distinct little flames were the manifold gifts coming from the one flaming Gift of God: the one same Spirit of the Father and the Son. Now he rests upon each of them, bright and warm, filling them with glory and peace — the glory and peace of Elijah on Horeb (cf. 1 Kgs 19:12), the glory and peace of the first Christmas (cf. Lk 2:14), the glory and peace of the Risen Christ (cf. Jn 20:21).

THE MOTHER OF THE CHURCH

I am the mother of fair love and of fear and of
knowledge and of holy hope. (Sir 24:24, Vulgate)

"AND they were all filled with the Holy Spirit"
(Acts 2:4). This was the immediate and enduring effect of Pentecost: a fullness of life — the life of
the Risen Christ — now poured out upon the earth and
destined to increase and multiply until the end of time.

Among those 120 faithful disciples was one — and
one only — who was already "full of grace." Immaculate from her conception, Mary of Nazareth was thus
enabled to cooperate with the Holy Spirit, who in the
fullness of time would come upon her to give birth to
the Seed of Eternal Life.

What began with her First-born Son thirty-three
years earlier is now to increase and multiply by her
same maternal cooperation to "the measure of the stature of the fullness of Christ" (Eph 4:13). At once a disciple of Jesus and his Mother, Our Lady is now enabled
by the Holy Spirit, her Spouse, to be at the same time
a member of the Church and Mother of the Church —
bearing in the Body of Christ all the children God has
given her (cf. Heb 2:13; Is 8:18).

"And they began to speak" (Acts 2:4). The last words
of Our Lady in Sacred Scripture were spoken in Cana
of Galilee (cf. Jn 2:5; the last Hail Mary of the Joyful
Mysteries). Her sorrows and her glories are both in
silence — the silence of perfect contemplation — and the
unique communication that a mother has with her children. A perfect instance of this communication is the
twenty-fourth chapter of the Book of Sirach: words of
wisdom, inspired by the Holy Spirit and appropriated
by the Church to Mary, her Mother.

ST. PETER

... Peter, standing with the eleven, lifted
up his voice... (Acts 2:14)

OUR Blessed Lady has, in the traditional picture of Pentecost, the central position. It is over her that the Spirit hovers, and it is her candle that is the first one lit. She has become once again the Mother: under her heart the life of the Church — the *Christus Totus* — begins. And from her heart that life is nourished, and will continue to be until the number of the elect, beginning with the 120, will be complete.

She, the holiest of God's creatures, is thus the exemplar and the channel of that first and ultimate purpose or mark of the Church: union with the triune God in holiness. Holy Mary and Holy Church are, in God's wondrous Providence, the same one "anointing," the same one Christ.

But notice now that from the tongues of fire enveloping all the disciples she does not speak to anyone outside that upper room, nor do any of the others — except the Twelve. And of the twelve Apostles one alone speaks to the world. Thus the concentric circles of disciples and Apostles issue in one voice: the voice of one man, speaking not by their choice but by Christ's. St. Peter, holder of the keys (cf. Mt 16:19) and feeder of the sheep (cf. Jn 21:17), is the Vicar of Christ, the Head of the Church.

As the holiness of the Church is entrusted to Mary the heart, so the unity of the Church is entrusted to Peter the head.

ST. PAUL

*. . . the Lord said to [Ananias], "Go, for [Saul is a
chosen instrument of mine, to carry my Name
to the Gentiles . . ." (Acts 9:11–14)*

T HE Acts of the Apostles has been called the "Gospel
of the Holy Spirit." Beginning in Jerusalem with
the Ascension of Our Lord and the Descent of the Holy
Spirit, it ends in Rome: the capital of the world and,
symbolically, the "end of the earth" (cf. Acts 1:8).

The Apostles whose "acts" are narrated are only two:
in the first half of the book, St. Peter, the first Apostle
(cf. Mt 10:2); and in the second half, St. Paul, the last
Apostle (cf. 1 Cor 15:8). These two are the Apostles *par
excellence*. Both are destined, beyond the conclusion of
St. Luke's book, to die in Rome.

They may be the two "witnesses" (i.e., martyrs)
described symbolically in the Apocalypse (Rev 11:3–13).
In any case, in historical fact they fulfill God's Providence regarding the first Holy City, Jerusalem, and bring
the Universal Church to the second Holy City, Rome.

Although St. Peter, as Christ's Vicar, first opened the
Church to the Gentiles — and thus made it Universal —
the real evangelization of the Gentiles was the work of
St. Paul (cf. Gal 2:3–9). He follows Peter — as *Catholicity*
follows Unity. As Peter is "the Rock," by Christ's direct
choice the prototype of the Oneness of the Church, so
St. Paul is "the Apostle," by Christ's direct choice the
prototype of the Catholicity of the Church.

This Universality of the Church is effectively present in the successors of St. Paul and all the other
Apostles: the bishops, in their "solicitude for all the
churches" (2 Cor 11:28), extending to all mankind to
the end of time.

THE SPIRIT OF TRUTH

*When the Spirit of Truth comes, he will
guide you into all the truth. (Jn 16:13)*

WITH Sts. Peter and Paul, we have indeed the two
divinely appointed prototypes respectively of the
Unity and the Catholicity of the Church. They stand,
as it were, on either side of Our Lady as in a sacred
triptych, for she is the prototype of the Holiness that
is the highest and most perfect mark of the Church.

But what of the fourth and last of the Church's
marks, her Apostolicity? Under that heading we include
the other Apostles, whose "acts" we must also remember, even though the Holy Spirit did not choose to
include them explicitly in that "fifth Gospel" written
by St. Luke. But implicitly their "acts" are there, form-
ing one organic whole with those of Sts. Peter and Paul.
This one organic whole we call the "Apostolic Tradition,"
flowing out across the centuries and the continents from
the Holy Spirit of Pentecost.

The first and fundamental part of the Apostolic Tradition is what the Apostles taught us to believe. The
words and deeds of Jesus revealing to us the Father were
sealed in the Apostles' memory and understanding by
the Holy Spirit, whom Jesus identified and introduced
to his Apostles as the "Spirit of Truth" (Jn 15:26).

He had already identified himself as the one Teacher
(Mt 23:10); indeed, he was in his very Person "the
Truth" (Jn 14:6). Now the "Spirit of Truth," that is,
his Spirit, is to lead them into all truth. And they, and
their successors, are to "hand on" this truth, and we
are to receive it in faith.

THE SPIRIT OF STRENGTH

*... with great power the Apostles gave their
testimony to the Resurrection of the Lord Jesus,
and great grace was upon them all... (Acts 4:33)*

THE Spirit of Truth, who is the Spirit of Jesus the Teacher, fulfilled what Our Lord had said at his Ascension both about himself and about his Apostles. "All power in heaven and on earth" was his (Mt 28:18), and as for them, they would be "clothed with power from on high" (Lk 24:49).

And as both St. Matthew and St. Luke conclude their Gospels on this "dynamic" note, so too does St. Mark. Flowing from the Apostles' faith, which is their possession of and witness to the truth, come all the "accompanying signs" of strength by which they will conquer the world (Mk 16:17–20).

Finally, St. John witnesses to this same truth: "this is the victory which conquers the world, our faith" (1 Jn 5:4). So from the truth of Christ the Teacher comes the strength of Christ the King, from faith comes hope.

This hope is surely the most characteristic note of the "acts" of the Apostles following Pentecost. How often are we told of their *parrhesia*: their "boldness," their "confidence," their "joy" (cf. Acts 4:13; 13:46; Rom 15:13; 2 Cor 10:2; Heb 10:35; 1 Pet 1:8)!

Yes, here is the hallmark of the Apostolic Tradition; twelve men setting out to conquer the world! Andrew to Scythia, Thomas to India, James to Spain. The written record is fragmentary, but the Tradition itself is sure. Out of hiddenness come signs, out of weakness comes strength, out of death comes resurrection, out of sorrow comes joy (cf. Jn 16:20).

One with Peter and "catholic" with Paul—and holy with Mary—the Apostles (and their successors), following in the Spirit of their King, will conquer the world!

THE SPIRIT OF LOVE

... God's love has been poured into our hearts through
the Holy Spirit who has been given to us. (Rom 5:5)

CHRIST the King, thorn-crowned and risen from the dead, gives to his Apostles — and through them to us — his Spirit of Strength. But that is not the end of his giving. The purpose of that strength — as of the truth from which it springs — is ultimately but one thing: to dispose us to receive his ultimate gift, the gift of his love.

From love alone came the whole "economy": Creation, Incarnation, Redemption. And for love and in love alone will it be fulfilled. This fulfillment is our Sanctification: our being made holy, our becoming one with God forever.

This ultimate gift of God is in fact God himself, for God is Love (1 Jn 4:8, 16). Now, this love which is God is proper to the Holy Spirit, for he is the mutual love and giving of the Father and the Son.

Just as it is in the Holy Spirit that the Father and the Son are one God, so it is in the same Holy Spirit that we become one with God. This first and ultimate work of the Holy Spirit in us is effected by the mediating sacrifice of Christ the Priest. Through him, with him, and in him, our exchange of gifts takes place.

If, as St. Ignatius reminds us in his "Contemplation for Obtaining Love," it is in action (more than in words) and in a mutual exchange of gifts that love exists,* then our loving God and our loving one another and our being loved by them is the one action of the Gift that is Jesus's Holy Spirit and ours.

---

* See Puhl, *The Spiritual Exercises of St. Ignatius*, nos. 230–31.

THE MYSTERY OF THE
DESCENT OF THE HOLY SPIRIT

*Hail Mary, full of grace, the Lord is with
thee, blessed art thou among women, and
blessed is the fruit of thy womb, Jesus.*

THE Third Glorious Mystery, the Mystery of the
Third Person of the Blessed Trinity and of Pentecost, is perhaps the most wondrous paradox in the
total paradox that is the Creed. So many seeming opposites at every turn! The utter clarity of its truth and its
obscurity, the mighty wind and the gentle breeze, the
innumerable charisms and the unique charity, the fire
and the water, the tongues and the silence, the objective and the subjective, the ardor and the peace. Seven
paradoxes? No! "Seventy times seven" (cf. Mt 18:22).

But only One is the Holy Spirit, who is at once the
"center" and the "circumference" of the Love that is God.

In the face of this Mystery, the tradition of the Faith
"that comes to us from the Apostles" (the Roman Canon)
teaches us to pray in the manner of St. Ignatius in his
Spiritual Exercises. More than once, his "Triple Colloquy"
bids us pray to Mary the Mother, thence to Jesus the Son,
thence to God the Father.*

Where, then, is the Holy Spirit? He is in us—he is
the "pray-er" (cf. Rom 8:26)! His praying in us in this
Mystery of the Rosary literally fulfills the "last word"
of Sacred Scripture. For he, "the Spirit," speaks jointly
with Mary, "the Bride," and together "the Spirit and
the Bride" say to Jesus: "Come" (Rev 22:17)!

*Holy Mary, Mother of God,
pray for us sinners, now and
at the hour of our death.
Amen.*

---

* Puhl, *The Spiritual Exercises of St. Ignatius*, nos. 67, 147.

THE FOURTH
GLORIOUS MYSTERY

✦

THE ASSUMPTION
OF OUR LADY

ST. JOHN

. . . [John] the disciple took [Mary] into his care.
(Jn 19:27)

A MONG all the Apostles, the "acts" of whom con-
stitute the "epilogue" of the Gospels (and therefore
of the Rosary), none is more to be remembered than
St. John. He occupies a unique position in the annals of
the early Church. On a par with Peter as "pillar" (cf.
Gal 2:9) and on a par with Paul as "theologian," John
outlived them both.

Indeed, he outlived all the Apostles, for "the saying
spread abroad among the brethren that this disciple was
not to die" (Jn 21:23). The "Benjamin" of the Twelve,
the "Beloved" of the Master and the recipient of the
inmost secrets of his Heart, this was the one chosen by
Jesus to be his replacement as "son" to his Mother (cf.
Jn 19:26). Among all the saints, except for St. Joseph,
John is the closest to Mary. Under his roof and care, we
contemplate the culmination of her earthly life.

One tradition has it that Our Lady lived out her days
in Ephesus, in a little house perched on a hill above the
city where, some three hundred years later, she would
be proclaimed the *Theotokos*: the "God-bearer."

But now in these golden years, while the Apostles
criss-crossed the Mediterranean founding the churches,
the Mother of the Church is close at hand to comfort
them, to be a "Paraclete" of good counsel and prayer.
Nothing is recorded for Sacred Scripture, nor need it be.
For all is confided in absolute trust, in silent watchful
solitude, to the cloistered safeguarding of her heart.

OUR LADY'S VIATICUM

*He brought me to the banqueting house, and
his banner over me was love. (Cant 2:4)*

HOW long was Our Lady's sojourn in this world
following Pentecost and the launching of the
Church? Sacred Scripture is silent, except for those
Lukan and Johannine intimations (cf. Lk 2:51; Jn 19:27),
which in the manner of the mustard seed (cf. Mt 13:31–
32) have nourished the piety of the faithful. Nor should
this manner of revelation surprise us, for it is totally
consistent with whatever little was written about her
under the inspiration of the Holy Spirit—whether in
the Hidden Life or in the Public Life or in the Paschal
Mystery of her Son.

It is all of a piece: the reserve and silence of ineffable
love bonding the hearts of Jesus and Mary.

It is surely no coincidence that the same reserve and
ineffability characterizes the Scriptural account of the
Holy Eucharist. How almost totally incidental is its
mention (cf. Jn 6; 1 Cor 10, 11), apart from the Last
Supper itself—and even then!

But how otherwise could it be for the "Mystery of
Faith"? For the "Mystery of Love"? Indeed, this had
to be the final phase of Our Lady's life.

While the Apostles went about the ministry of the
Word that was Our Lord's commission to them, the
widowed Mother of Jesus "did not depart from the temple, worshiping with fasting and prayer night and day"
(Lk 2:37). The Temple of the New Testament is his
Body, his Eucharist. This Body that came from her is
now once more within her, in a Communion and peace
that surpasses understanding (cf. Phil 4:7).

Here is her very life, her anticipation of heaven, her
Viaticum.

OUR LADY'S DORMITION

... to me to live is Christ, and to die is gain. (Phil 1:21)

ON the highest point of Mount Sion in Jerusalem, not far from the Cenacle, stands the "Church of the Dormition," a relatively modern dome-like structure, marking the site where, according to a venerable tradition, Our Lady "fell asleep."

More than any other person (including her son John, cf. Jn 21:23), St. Paul's dilemma had been preeminently hers: "Christ will be honored in my body, whether by life or by death. For to me to live is Christ, and to die is gain.... Yet which I shall choose I cannot tell. I am hard pressed between the two. My desire is to depart and be with Christ, for that is far better" (Phil 1:20–23).

As always, her choice was God's choice; so now by the Father's will, whether mediated by her request or by other circumstances, St. John brought her back to the Holy City, there to die where her Son Jesus had died. Like Jesus, death was not her debt to pay. Rather, for her, immaculate Daughter of Sion, death was the prize, the pearl, the bond, the seal, the consummation of her heart's desire — and his.

And so "the time came for her to be delivered" (Lk 2:6). Now, besides being one with Jesus in her Viaticum, she would be one with all her other children in tasting death. We may see her as imaged in that church, lying in state before the altar. The Apostles, concelebrating her Requiem, sing her *Magnificat*, the canticle which, from that time to this, is the Church's "Evensong."

THE ASSUMPTION OF OUR LADY

Arise, my love, my fair one, and come away;
for lo! The winter is past, the rain is over and
gone. The flowers appear on the earth, the
time of singing has come. (Cant 2:10−12)

THE Mother Church of Jerusalem venerates Our Lady's "falling asleep" on the heights of Sion. So too the Church venerates her place of burial in the valley beneath the Temple Mount, not far from where her Son Jesus entered into his Passion.

But the virginal body of God's Mother was not to be there for long. Legend has it that on the third day, the Apostles found her tomb empty. As always, in life and in death, Mary links us with Jesus: she follows him, and we follow her.

The recognition of the essential fact of her resurrection does not arise from pious sentiment or theological argument; neither legends nor syllogisms ground our faith. It is, rather, the "sense of the Faith"—that "anointing" about which St. John wrote (cf. 1 Jn 2:27), which in due time, under the guidance of the Holy Spirit, induced the Universal Church's solemn definition that "the Immaculate Mother of God, Mary ever-Virgin, when the course of her earthly life was finished, was taken up body and soul into the glory of heaven."*

Our Lady's Assumption into heaven is infallibly true, uniting, as it does, the truths of Our Lord's Resurrection and our own (cf. 1 Cor 15:16). As always with Mary, her glories are for Jesus, her First-born—and for us, her other children.

But now all of us, including Jesus, may contemplate that glory of ours—in her. See her now, the "Assumpta," the "One Taken up"—the one perfect creature, the one perfectly redeemed, the one perfectly made holy.

Oh, "Virgin of virgins, our Mother!"

---

* *Munificentissimus Deus* 44.

OUR LADY AND
THE BLESSED TRINITY

*...from him and through him and to him are all
things. To him be glory forever. (Rom 11:36)*

FOR this last and culminating Marian mystery, it
is important to note that the word used habitu-
ally by Tradition, and officially by the Magisterium, is
"Assumption." Unlike Our Lord's "Ascension," which
means "going up" to heaven in an active sense, Our
Lady's "Assumption" is passive: she is "assumed,"
"taken up" by God, body and soul, into glory.

Her being "taken" by God was, of course, first
known by her before it was known by the Church. In
her *Magnificat* she rejoices in God her Savior, "who has
done great things" for her (Lk 1:49). Her only "action"
is her *fiat*: "let it be done to me according to thy word"
(Lk 1:38).

Now, face to face, she sees God as he sees himself, in
the Mystery of mysteries: Father, Son, and Holy Spirit
in the one being, the one knowing, and the one loving
that is the One True God.

The Assumpta was then and is now and will be
forever the one person uniquely related to the Three
Persons who are God. Unique Daughter of the Father,
unique Mother of the Son, unique Spouse of the Spirit,
Mary knows and loves God not only more in degree than
all other creatures combined; her knowledge and love
are different in kind from theirs. For God, in a manner
beyond our understanding, made himself dependent on
her! She "completes" him by giving him Jesus!

Now in heaven by his side, she sees the triune God.
Yes, with and through her Jesus, her *Magnificat* says it
all: "Holy is his Name!" (Lk 1:49).

OUR LADY AND THE ANGELS

Bless the Lord, all you his angels, you mighty
ones who do his will. (Ps 102/103:21)

THE "holy" of Our Lady's *Magnificat* is now
echoed by the "Holy, Holy, Holy" of the angels.
For now, "in heaven as it was on earth," by a kind of
wondrous inversion of the *Pater Noster*'s injunction, the
angels, who from the first day of creation had begun
their ceaseless prayer of praise before the throne of the
triune God, now finally attain the object of their long
desire (cf. 1 Pet 1:12). They now at last have in their
midst a created person purer and mightier than they,
one in whom God is totally pleased, so that now it can
no longer be said that the heavens are not clean in his
sight (cf. Job 15:15).

Satan and his cohorts had been conquered by St.
Michael, yes, and expelled from heaven (cf. Rev 12:7–10).
But Satan's head remained uncrushed until the woman
assumed by God himself had come (cf. Gen 3:15)!

See her now, as Christian art has always seen her,
escorted by myriads of angels into Paradise. But these
hosts of heaven owe more to her than she to them.
For only because of her are they still "ascending" (cf.
Jn 1:51) — lifted higher, even beyond their angelic nature,
to contemplate their Creator and Lord in his Manhood,
the fruit of her womb.

Yes, himself "lifted up," Jesus draws all to himself —
first his Mother and then his angels (cf. Jn 12:32). But do
not see them only as a cloud, or even as "choirs." They
are all distinct persons — among whom is the one angel
destined to be my Guardian, destined to lead me home
to Jesus and Mary.

OUR LADY AND THE SAINTS

*... behold a great multitude which no man
can number... standing before the throne
and before the Lamb... (Rev 7:9)*

IN his Paschal Mystery Our Lord had visited his
saints in Limbo, and then he brought their souls
home to heaven with himself. Now, with his Mother
assumed body and soul into heaven, we can say that
just as what was lacking in his Passion is completed by
his saints (cf. Col 1:24), so too what was lacking in his
Resurrection is completed by them — and primarily so
in the person of his Mother.

For she is the one person totally redeemed, the prototype of the Passover prepared for all mankind. Totally
present in heaven in body and soul, Mary is the very
heart of the Communion of the Saints.

In her person, body and soul, the Old and New Testa-
ments merge into one completed Covenant between God
and the human race. For she is at once the Daughter of
Sion and the Mother of the Church.

Having given Jesus with herself to God, she is now
given back by him to "her people." First, to all those
souls awaiting her arrival in heaven, from Adam and
Eve on down to her own lifetime on earth: Sts. Joachim and Anne, St. Joseph and St. John Baptist, Dismas
the Good Thief, and St. Stephen and St. James, John's
brother (cf. Acts 12:2).

Then, on to the end of time she awaits the rest of
the children as, one by one, across the continents and
centuries, they come home to her. The Apostles and
the Martyrs, the canonized and the uncanonized, the
known and the unknown, whoever is now or will ever
be in heaven is there because of her.

OUR LADY AND
THE SOULS IN PURGATORY

If any man's work is burned up, he will
suffer loss, though he himself will be saved,
but only as through fire. (1 Cor 3:15)

SO far, we have contemplated Our Lady in heaven glorying in the embrace of the triune God and in the fellowship of his angels and saints. Her prayer is one of pure praise and gratitude, her *Magnificat* renewed in the unending vision of God, her Savior, her Jesus.

In such a vision and prayer, is there still room for the prayer that was also hers on earth, the prayer of intercession and petition? Is she not mindful of her Son's own prayer of intercession, right there in heaven, renewing with his unhealable wounds his blessed Passion (cf. Heb 7:25)?

No, she is even more than she was on earth, the vigilant mother. Mother of Sorrows until the end of time, until the number of the elect is complete (cf. Rev 6:11), she sees now with the utter clarity of heaven the darkness in the cosmos. On the little planet earth, all through the mysterious distances between, she sees that "they have no wine" (Jn 2:3).

The children claiming the first attention of Mary's heart may well be those who are so near and yet so far from heaven: the souls in Purgatory. For indeed, what souls are so poor as they!—the forgotten dead (cf. Ps 30/31:12), the ones utterly unable to help themselves (cf. Job 19:21), the last and least of the brethren (cf. Mt 25:40).

And so to these little ones, now all the littler in their humbled privation and longing, the most gracious Advocate turns her eyes of mercy. On those "half-alive" souls she pours the wine of her maternal care (cf. Lk 10:30, 34). And in due time, that wine will become the saving Blood of the Sacred Heart.

OUR LADY AND OURSELVES

Hail Holy Queen, Mother of mercy....
To thee do we cry, poor banished children of Eve. *

THAT Our Lady, Mother and model of the Church, should be so attentive to the Poor Souls in Purgatory may sometimes be for us a matter of quiet reproach. Are they not, after all, assured of heaven? There is no doubt whatever of their eventual release! Why can't they be more patient, then, and turn their eyes toward us, the living, whose assurance of eternal life is still at issue?

Yet, earthbound as we are, we must not let the vapors arising from this "valley of tears" obscure our vision. But then again, isn't there something perhaps providential in this "present darkness" of ours, veiling as it does the stark reality of those "spiritual hosts of wickedness" (Eph 6:12) that engulf this errant planet and would, if unveiled, tempt us to despair?

As the little time-trapped creatures that we are, we must be grateful for the paradox that is the grace of our present life. Vulnerable as we are from the unsureness of our ultimate salvation, we yet should know that that unsureness is from our part and not from God's!

Where our sinfulness abounds, his grace yet more abounds (cf. Rom 5:20). And out of that superabundance of grace comes the revelation of the one whom the Church Militant invokes as "our life, our sweetness and our hope."

Yes, "full of grace" from her place in heaven, she does see me, not as a tiny speck in the cosmos but as her child, whose uniqueness absorbs all her maternal attention. The totality of the Church Triumphant, Suffering, and Militant, and the totality of "me" — both totalities are totally hers.

---

* *Salve Regina.*

THE MYSTERY OF THE
ASSUMPTION OF OUR LADY

*Hail Mary, full of grace, the Lord is with
thee, blessed art thou among women, and
blessed is the fruit of thy womb, Jesus.*

THE Fourth Glorious Mystery is not the "end" of
the Rosary. It is nearly so, and in a certain sense
it is so. What could be more of a "finality" (for that is
what "end" in its "final" sense means) for the Blessed
Virgin Mary than her being "taken up" by God into a
place totally unique, at the very apex of the universe
and enclosed (as it were) in the Blessed Trinity itself?

That is why August 15 is not only her greatest solemnity; it is in a sense her only one! For its object is to
celebrate the reality of Mary, not in this or that facet of
it in time or space, but in its very self, in the timelessness
and spacelessness of its being "here" and "now."

Yes, this transcendent, this "meta-historical" glory
of Our Lady must not in any way distance her from
us, or us from her. For, after Christ's sacred humanity
(and because of it), she is at once the closest to God and
the closest to us.*

She is indeed closest to us where we are, here and
now, on earth. She comes to us, not from her Assumption but in it (cf. Prov 8:30–31). This final "glory" is the
Fifth and final Mystery of the original Rosary.

*Holy Mary, Mother of God,
pray for us sinners, now and
at the hour of our death.
Amen.*

---

* See *Lumen Gentium* 54.

THE FIFTH
GLORIOUS MYSTERY

✠

THE CORONATION
OF OUR LADY

OUR LADY IN THE CHURCH'S HISTORY

... a great sign appeared in heaven, a woman clothed
with the sun, with the moon beneath her feet, and
on her head a crown of twelve stars. (Rev 12:1)

AT the very center of the Book of Revelation, that
mysterious culmination of the Sacred Scriptures,
there occurs a vision of "a great sign in heaven": a
Woman surrounded by sun, moon, and stars. Here is
the Scripturally inspired culmination of the Rosary: the
Coronation of Mary, Mother of the Messiah, Mother
and Model of the Church.

The Church Triumphant — yes, for she is already
in heaven with her Son. Yet also, since this is the one
Church Universal — and therefore also the Church Militant and Pilgrim — she is still here on earth. In fact, as
the vision continues, she is "in the wilderness, where
she has a place prepared by God" (Rev 12:6). There she
will be "nourished for a time and times and half a time"
(Rev 12:14) by the prayers of "the rest of her offspring":
her children who, by her nourishing prayers in turn,
will continue "to keep the commandments of God and
bear testimony to Jesus" (Rev 12:17).

Just as all history — of the Church and of the world —
is encapsulated in this one chapter of Sacred Scripture,
and just as that same history is, as St. Augustine tells us,
the proper object of catechesis, let us now in this decade
recall "the more striking occurrences, which ... have
taken a standing as cardinal points of the history" *: the
history of Our Lady's sojourn with her children in exile.

The "ancient serpent's" enmity toward her (cf.
Gen 3:15) has grown only greater across the ages — for
he is now a "dragon," spewing against her a deluge of
defiance (cf. Rev 12:15–16). Yet all the powers of darkness cannot dim the stars that are her crown.

---

* E. Phillips Barker, trans., *A Treatise of Saint Aurelius Augus-*
tine, Bishop of Hippo: On the Catechizing of the Uninstructed
(Methuen & Co., 1912), 7.

OUR LADY AND
THE ROMAN CHURCH

Hail, Holy Mother, who didst bring forth the King,
who ruleth over heaven and earth forever and ever. *

IF now, in this "time and times and half a time" until the Parousia when Christ himself will come again in glory, Our Lady anticipates that coming—as prophesized by St. John in his Apocalypse—where in this "wilderness" of earth has she first appeared?

Her first recorded recognition as the "New Eve," true "Mother of the Living," following the intimation of the Scriptures, came within a century of the Apostles, in the writings of St. Justin and St. Irenaeus. Following St. Peter and St. Paul, who with their *Quo vadis?* were themselves following the suffering Christ, both of these ancient Fathers came from the East to Rome. There, after the early successors of St. Peter had displaced the later successors of Caesar as the rulers of the Eternal City, the first official sanctuary in the Patriarchate of the West honoring Our Lady was dedicated on the highest of Rome's seven hills: the Patriarchal Basilica of "St. Mary Major" on the Esquiline.

The origin of this basilica as coming like snow in August is legendary, but its dedication less than a century later is factual. It occurred right after the Council of Ephesus in the early fifth century. Its golden mosaics portraying Our Lady's coronation highlight its status as the world's oldest and greatest extant Marian shrine.

And fittingly so, for if the Church as Universal is our Mother, then equally so is the Church as Roman! Indeed, "Catholic" and "Roman" are correlative terms: one cannot be strictly true without the other. We children of the Holy Father have Mary with absolute certainty as our Mother, and the best name for our family home is—Rome.

---

* Entrance Antiphon, Common of Our Lady, #1.

OUR LADY OF MOUNT CARMEL

... by the help of her prayers may we come
to the mountain which is Christ...*

A PROVIDENTIAL fact of history is that the earliest extant sanctuary of Our Lady in the whole Catholic world is her "Major" Basilica in Rome. But that must not obscure the antecedent fact that, as in all other essential matters of the Catholic Church, what is Roman was originally from the East — from the Holy Land.

The Holy City, first and last, is Jerusalem; God's promise to the patriarchs and the prophets is irrevocable. No wonder, then, that our Mother Church of the West has always looked with nostalgia toward "the Orient from on high" as her Mother.

And where in the Holy Land would her Mother be more aptly honored than on that immemorial height of holiness: the Mount of Carmel! There, in unbroken continuity from Elijah, the One True God is worshiped. And never more faithfully so than by the disciples of Jesus, Son of Mary, who taught them to worship "in spirit and in truth" (Jn 4:23).

Thus it was that in the High Middle Ages when Western Christendom, emulating Elijah's zeal, regained the Holy Land; the perhaps greatest enduring treasure of her Crusade was the Carmelite tradition of contemplative prayer. Greater than the glorious cathedrals and universities that flowered across Europe in that medieval springtime were the seeds of grace, maternally nourished by Mary under her title of Our Lady of Mount Carmel.

Then, as always, in God's good time, her days of waiting would be fulfilled, and from such hidden places as Avila and Lisieux the indefectible life of Holy Church would be renewed.

---

* Opening prayer of the Mass for Our Lady of Mount Carmel.

OUR LADY OF GUADALUPE

Who is this that looks forth like the dawn, fair
as the moon, bright as the sun, terrible as
an army with banners? (Cant 6:10)

IT is now some three centuries later, and the towering achievements of the medieval West have subsided, even down to internal disruption. A would-be Reformation threatens the very survival of the Catholic Church.

It is a "time and times and half a time" all over again, when no longer, it seems, would the indefectible Church be able to withstand the infidel incursions of Islam (the conquerors of Carmel!), beset as she is by rebellious heretics from within her fold, who in their rebellion invoked the Christ but not his Mother.

And as though to compound the chaos of that tumultuous time, the princes of Christendom — and especially the Catholic kings — are distracted over the glory and gold of conquest in a New World. "From evening isles fantastical rings faint the Spanish gun . . ."*

Then, as out of nowhere, comes heaven's intervention. On the site of a pagan Aztec shrine on the hill of Tepeyac, near the capital city of Mexico, Our Lady appears to a poor middle-aged native, bidding him go to the bishop to have him build on this very site a sanctuary for the Mother of the One True God. As proof, she gives him her portrait: a miraculous photograph — beautifully gracious, sublimely serene, young and with child!

For the bishop and his Franciscan brothers, as for the now St. Juan Diego — and for all the succeeding generations of the faithful — this sacred image is the pledge of Our Lady's presence among us, in the very center of the New World, redressing the balance of the Old!

---

* G. K. Chesterton, *Lepanto* (Ignatius Press, 2003), 11.

OUR LADY OF LOURDES

O my dove, in the clefts of the rock, in the covert of the cliff, let me see your face, let me hear your voice, for your voice is sweet, and your face is comely. (Cant 2:14)

A NOTHER three centuries have passed, and the "modern" world presaged by the Renaissance and the Enlightenment is now "established" by the great Revolution given its birth by the "eldest daughter of the Church," France. Such are the ironies of history — or rather the implications of the Apocalypse — that the greatest challenge to "the Woman" should come, not from the morning lands of the infidel in the East, nor from the evening lands of the pagan in the West, but from the noonday lands of a thousand-year-old Christendom centered in the France of "Notre Dame."

And so it was that, as so often before, the response of heaven to the errancies of earth was a Visitation once more of the Mother of the One True God. In a grotto beside a mountain stream, the *Damoiselle* appeared to a little peasant girl named Bernadette, and identified herself as "the Immaculate Conception."

What a response to the cult of "the brave new world" that was then the dreamy fantasy of time-worn Europe! Lourdes came almost immediately to be, and has always remained thereafter, the very prototype and standard of any authentic Marian apparition. Our Lady must appear "in the clefts of the rock, in the covert of the cliff" (Cant 2:14); she must offer "a garden fountain, a well of living water and flowing streams" (Cant 4:15).

These are the sacramentals of salvation, the elements that will outlast "modernity." They enshrine the "Immaculata," "the fairest of women" (Cant 6:1), "the seal upon our hearts" (Cant 8:6).

Here at her feet, with roses, is the world's peace.

OUR LADY AND "TODAY"

*... exhort one another every day, as long as
it is called "today," that none of you may
be hardened by the deceitfulness of sin. For
we share in Christ, if only we hold our first
confidence firm to the end. (Heb 3:13–14)*

WITH four Hail Marys (corresponding to the four dates in the Church's calendar honoring a "local" Marian title), we have traversed Our Lady's history since her Assumption, and we have seen that it has been a Visitation: heaven and earth are as one!

Indeed, both leading to and flowing from the Eucharistic Holy Communion itself, the Communion of the Saints is most fittingly signified and caused by a Marian mediation: the enduring motherhood of the Church personified in Mary. She makes us saints, that is, one with Jesus.

But this making takes time — and that time is right now in this present moment. "Today" we are saints only in hope. To us, still in this world of time, what must be our prayer to her now as we near the end of our Rosary?

There is perhaps no better prayer than the one that St. Ignatius proposes in his very first mention of Our Lady in his *Spiritual Exercises.* * He introduces her as my Mediatrix, praying to her Son (the Mediator) to obtain for me from his Father a triple grace (the Holy Spirit!), namely: (1) to know my sins, that I may hate them; (2) to know the disorder of my life, that I may amend it; and (3) to know the "world" as it really is, in its own eyes that I may condemn it, and in God's eyes that I may pity it.

This triple "purgative" prayer to Our Lady is most appropriate to this "now," this present moment of our lives. Until we die, we are sinners, and she who mothered him who "became sin" for us knows us today for her own.

---

* Puhl, *The Spiritual Exercises of St. Ignatius*, no. 63.

OUR LADY OF THE WAY

*... in me is all grace of the way and of truth, in me
is all hope of life and of virtue. (Sir 24:25, Vulgate)*

T HE "today" that is the present moment (this very
 Rosary that I am now praying) will pass away, as
has the past. But that which will not pass away is that
future which is eternity.

Important as the present is, it is so only in function of
what it leads me to. I must see my life on earth only as
a "way." So much, indeed, is this so that from the very
beginning the Church has called her life "the way" (cf.
Acts 9:2; 19:9; 22:4, 14, 22). Her "way" is simply "Jesus,"
for he is "the Way" (his humanity) to "the Truth and
the Life" (his divinity) (Jn 14:4–6).

And the "grace of the way" — that is, its being given
to us — is in and through Mary, his Mother and ours.

On this earth and in time — then, now, and always
until its end — this Marian and ecclesial "way," which
is Jesus, is the Way of the Cross (cf. Lk 9:23; Heb 12:1–2;
13:12–13). And as our prayer for this "grace of the way,"
let us use once more the great "triple colloquy" that St.
Ignatius loved so much that he repeated it as the centerpiece of his *Spiritual Exercises.* * He bids us first beg of
Our Lady the grace to be admitted under the Standard
of Jesus in poverty and suffering. (This is once more her
mediation with Jesus, who in turn exercises once more
his mediation with God the Father.)

This is indeed the "grace of the way" — at once purgative and illuminative and unitive, at once the "high"
way of La Storta and the "little" way of Lisieux, the
one and only way of the Holy Cross. For here alone is
Jesus as "he who is": God and Man, Crucified and Risen,
our *Viaticum Vitae.*

---

* Puhl, *The Spiritual Exercises of St. Ignatius*, no. 147.

OUR DEATH

... it is appointed unto men once to die... (Heb 9:27)

A S our Rosary nears its end, it may be well to note how quickly that end has come. "Today" was two Hail Marys past, and in the Hail Mary following it we had "the Way" — to what? Is that "Way" now completed, and are we now already in the future? No, but in "a little while" we will be (cf. Jn 16:16).

The Hail Mary in the Joyful Mysteries corresponding to this present one (i.e., reflection 48) contemplated St. Joseph's death, and the corresponding Hail Mary in the Sorrowful Mysteries (i.e., reflection 98) contemplated Our Lord's death.

We contemplated both deaths with Our Lady, who was present at them both. Now with her still, we contemplate our own death — or rather my death, for each of us dies alone. Yet, in that aloneness I turn to her, a turning that I have anticipated in every Hail Mary when I said to her: "pray for me a sinner at the hour of my death. Amen."

Yes, as a "sinner" I die, for death is the punishment for sin. Death is meant to be mysterious, awesome both in its universality and in its uniqueness: its being "once and for all."

Yet, for St. Joseph, Our Lady, and all the saints, death was, not in spite of but because of its mystery, something to be desired! For the real mystery of death is, first and last, made intelligible (and therefore desirable) only in Christ. His Death is my life (cf. Rom 14:78; Phil 1:21; 1 Thess 5:9–10)!

So, as a forgiven sinner I can die; thus, I turn to my Mother now, anticipating the hour of my death. Amen.

OUR RESURRECTION

... that I may know [Christ] and the power of his Resurrection, and may share his sufferings, becoming like him in his death, that if possible I may attain the resurrection from the dead. (Phil 3:10–11)

"AFTER death the judgment" (Heb 9:27). That judgment is God's, but it is also mine (cf. Jn 3:18–21). In eternity, I will simply ratify God's judgment of me — for good or ill — for I will see myself as he sees me.

And in this truth, which is God, I will through all eternity remain. This truth and this eternity begin when I die, for they were "realized" — that is, made effective — when he died in the Person of his Incarnate Son upon the Cross. That is why the Good Thief was "this very day" brought by Jesus into Paradise (Lk 23:43).

And if I die as the Good Thief died — in Christ's death — then I am living in him: in his sanctifying grace, which is his life and mine. It will be but a matter of time, the duration of which is nothing when compared to eternity (cf. 2 Pet 3:8), before I too will rise in his Resurrection — when he "will change my lowly body to be like his glorious body, by the power which enables him to subject all things to himself" (Phil 3:21).

Thus, by a "plenary indulgence" of his merciful love, time itself — however measured — will be no more, and our whole self, soul and body, will enter into Jesus — as on this earth he entered into us in his Holy Communion — to become the *Christus Totus*.

Both enterings are related to Mary, the Mother of all the Living. Just as in a sense she was our earth, so too in a sense she is our heaven.

OUR LADY OF THE ROSARY

Mystical Rose, pray for us....
Queen of the Most Holy Rosary, pray for us. *

IN the last two Hail Marys we have had a glimpse of our own individual Paschal Mystery awaiting us. It is the culmination of our "way," which is the following of Jesus and Mary and all the saints into the Communion in heaven, which is our destiny.

In this present Hail Mary, which completes our Rosary, we may fittingly note that this completed Rosary is at this moment the very last installment in that immense pool of prayer that has been but one great Rosary across the ages.

Our Rosary is now linked with St. Pius V's at the moment of Lepanto, out of which came the liturgical celebration of Our Lady of the Rosary. It is now also linked with the Rosary that St. Pius X must have prayed the moment he heard of Sarajevo, out of which came something to do with Our Lady's appearance three years later at Fatima.

What happened at Fatima may well be the greatest single attested miracle in the history of the Church; it was surely the "sign of the times," the overture to the Apocalypse that was the twentieth century.

Where we go from here — including our own individual Paschal Mystery as an integral part of the whole — is in the hands of God. Our Rosary, poor and little as it has been, is now in the hands of Mary, linked with her Rosary that she brought from heaven.

There is now but one Rosary — the crown about her heart.

---

* Litany of Loretto.

THE MYSTERY OF THE CORONATION OF OUR LADY

Hail Mary, full of grace, the Lord is with thee, blessed art thou among women, and blessed is the fruit of thy womb, Jesus.

THE "Corona"—the crown that is the Rosary—is now complete. From a seed that is its beginning, through a thorn that is its stem, to a rose that is its completion, it is truly a sign of the Trinity in Unity that is our "all in all": the Mystery of God in the Mystery of his Christ.

This completion of our Rosary resembles the completion of St. Ignatius's *Spiritual Exercises*: his *Contemplatio ad Amorem*—a contemplation meant to bring heaven to earth (God in all his creatures) and earth to heaven (all his creatures in God).*

So we have contemplated—and will forever contemplate—the Mystery of the Creature who is God: Our Lord Jesus Christ. And we do so in the mysteries that he shared first with his Mother and now with us.

The *Catechism of the Catholic Church* puts in effect all these mysteries into three: the Revelation, the Redemption, and the Recapitulation (nos. 516–18). Here are the seed, the thorn, and the rose that are the joys, the sorrows, and the glories of Our Lady: the Immaculata, the Dolorosa, and the Assumpta—Maria!

Holy Mary, Mother of God, pray for us sinners, now and at the hour of our death. Amen.

---

* See Puhl, *The Spiritual Exercises of St. Ignatius*, nos. 230–37.

ABOUT THE AUTHOR

FATHER ROBERT IGNATIUS BRADLEY, S.J., born on May 15, 1924, began his long journey to the priesthood at the age of three, when he asked his parents, Joseph and Muriel Bradley of Spokane, WA, to give him everything he needed to "celebrate Mass" as his birthday present. His father's friend, a woodworker, carved an eight inch tall chalice and a paten and painted them gold, while the mother of newly-appointed Spokane Bishop Charles D. White sewed the altar cloth and vestments, making them a little large so he could grow into them. His mother baked "communion hosts" and provided grape juice, altar candles, and a Missal.

And so, on May 15, 1927, with two older brothers drafted as altar boys, and the large family and friends gathered in makeshift pews, the future Fr. Bradley solemnly "celebrated" his first "Mass." According to family legend, the sermon was targeted at the misdeeds of his four older brothers and lasted quite a long time. The chalice and paten still remain as a family treasure.

As he progressed through St. Augustine School and Gonzaga High School, Fr. Bradley shared duties with his brothers as altar boys for Bishop White's daily Masses at his residence. Two weeks after graduating from Gonzaga in 1941, he followed his older brother Richard into the Society of Jesus. On August 15, 1955, Fr. Bradley was ordained to the priesthood in Louvain, Belgium, beginning his journey first as a priest serving the people of God but also as a renowned scholar and professor in the Jesuit tradition.

The Oregon Province of the Society of Jesus sent him to Columbia University to study for a doctorate in history, and then assigned him to teach history at Seattle University. He was promoted to dean of the College of Arts and Sciences but found administrative work unsuitable. He wanted to be in the classroom, and so upon the invitation of Fr. John Hardon, S. J., he joined the faculty of a new catechetical institute at St. John's University in New York, where he taught theology.

While at St. John's, Fr. Bradley became the chaplain of a new organization founded in the wake of Vatican Council II, Catholics United for the Faith. He served CUF for thirty-five years, writing many articles for *Lay Witness* magazine, conducting retreats, and providing spiritual guidance. He also wrote many articles and book reviews for *Homiletic and Pastoral Review*, and contributed chapters to the new *Catholic Encyclopedia* and several books on theology and catechetics.

In 1983, Father joined the faculty of the Notre Dame Pontifical Catechetical Institute in Arlington, VA, now the Notre Dame Graduate School of Christendom College in Front Royal, VA. He taught many courses in theology to graduate students as well as candidates for the diaconate in the Diocese of Arlington.

A sabbatical took Fr. Bradley to Rome in the mid-1980s to work on a Doctorate in Sacred Theology (STD) at the Pontifical University of St. Thomas Aquinas (the Angelicum), which he received in 1988. Upon resuming his duties at the Notre Dame Institute, he also became the chaplain for the Poor Clare Monastery in Alexandria, VA, serving the cloistered sisters for ten years.

Not one to ever be idle, Father co-authored a translation of *The Roman Catechism* (Pauline Books & Media, 1986) with Monsignor Eugene Kevane, lectured at conferences on the Rosary and the Blessed Mother, conducted retreats, and served as chaplain for the Legion of Mary in Northern Virginia. During the summers, he was the director of Our Lady of Peace Catechetical Institute in Beaverton, OR. Fr. Bradley also authored *The Roman Catechism in the Catechetical Tradition of the Church* (Rowman & Littlefield, 1990).

He moved to his mother's home state of Texas in 1996, where he accepted an adjunct faculty position in theology at the University of Dallas Institute for Religious and Pastoral Studies and also served as adjunct faculty at Our Lady of Guadalupe Seminary of the Fraternal Society of St. Peter (FSSP) in Denton, Nebraska. Assigned by the bishop of Austin to pastoral work, Fr. Bradley was the celebrant for the weekly liturgies of the St. Joseph Latin Mass Society at St. Mary Cathedral, until he became ill in late 2011. He also served as chaplain to the Legion of Mary in Austin, offered lectures in theology for the laity, and worked individually with students from the University of Texas-Austin who wished to enter the Catholic Church.

On December 20, 2013, Fr. Bradley went home to God. He is buried in the Jesuit Cemetery in Spokane near his older brother Fr. Richard S. Bradley, S.J.